WORKERS
WITHOUT
FRONTIERS

WORKERS WITHOUT FRONTIERS

THE IMPACT OF GLOBALIZATION ON INTERNATIONAL MIGRATION

Peter Stalker

LYNNE RIENNER PUBLISHERS

145418

Published in the United States of America in 2000 by
Lynne Rienner Publishers, Inc.
1800 30th Street, Boulder, Colorado 80301
www.rienner.com
ISBN 1-55587-856-3 (cloth, Rienner)
ISBN 1-55587-881-4 (paper, Rienner)

and in the United Kingdom by
Lynne Rienner Publishers, Inc.
3 Henrietta Street, Covent Garden, London WC2E 8LU

Published in Switzerland in 2000 by the
International Labour Office
CH-1211 Geneva-22, Switzerland
www.ilo.org/publns
ISBN 92-2-111383-3 (cloth, ILO)
ISBN 92-2-110854-6 (paper, ILO)

Library of Congress Cataloging-in-Publication Data
Stalker, Peter.
   Workers without frontiers : the impact of globalization on
international migration / Peter Stalker.
   Includes bibliographical references and index.
   1. Alien labor. 2. Emigration and immigration—Economic aspects.
3. International economic relations. I. Title.
HD6300.S734   2000
331'.6'2—dc21   99-37487
                                                          CIP
British Cataloguing in Publication Data
A Cataloguing in Publication record for this book
is available from the British Library.

The designations employed in ILO publications, which are in conformity with United
Nations practice, and the presentation of material therein do not imply the expression of
any opinion whatsoever on the part of the International Labour Office concerning the
legal status of any country, area, or territory or of its authorities, or concerning the delim-
itation of its frontiers.
   The responsibility for opinions expressed in studies and other contributions rests
solely with their authors, and publication does not constitute an endorsement by the
International Labour Office of the opinions expressed in them.
   Reference to names of firms and commercial products and processes does not imply
their endorsement by the International Labour Office, and any failure to mention a particular firm, commercial product, or process is not a sign of disapproval.
   Publications of the International Labour Office enjoy copyright under Protocol 2 of
the Universal Copyright Convention. Nevertheless, short excerpts from them may be
reproduced without authorization, on condition that the source is indicated. For rights
of reproduction or translation, application should be made to the Publications Bureau
(Rights and Permissions), International Labour Office, CH-1211 Geneva 22, Switzerland.
The International Labour Office welcomes such applications.

Printed and bound in the United States of America

5 4 3 2 1

Contents

Illustrations

Box

Foreword

Of the many questions raised by globalization, one that has seized the ILO's attention is how it would affect the mobility of workers across state frontiers and whether existing labor institutions would be sufficient to safeguard their fundamental rights. Most predictions point to a much higher scale of labor mobility in the twenty-first century, not because of liberalization of immigration controls, but because of growing labor supply pressures, rising income inequalities within and across nations brought about by globalization itself, and the revolution in information and communication technologies. Given the lack of universal acceptance of the case for unrestricted immigration, there are concerns that bigger numbers of migrants would be undocumented and that labor institutions that have evolved to meet national needs would be inadequate to provide for the social protection and security of globally mobile work forces.

This book brings together the findings and conclusions of empirical studies by the ILO and many others on how greater integration of capital and commodity markets may have reduced or further widened income disparities between nations and among groups within them. It examines whether reducing poverty is likely to dampen people's propensity to emigrate, and whether in a more integrated global economy the prospects for development of poor states would be helped or undermined by the impact of migration on their labor markets. These are timely issues for the international community to address as we search for the means to manage growth better in the face of highly volatile capital markets. The recent financial crises in Asia and Latin America remind us of how quickly social and economic gains can be wiped out by external shocks, and how much of the costs of adjustments are, in the final counting, borne by workers.

The book is disturbing in its conclusion that the evidence so far available on the impact of globalization points to a likely worsening of migration pressures in many parts of the world. Peter Stalker finds that processes integral to globalization have intensified the disruptive effects of modernization and capitalist development. While acknowledging that this has been different from one country to another, "the general effect has been a crisis of economic security." Indeed, available evidence indicates that the integration of world markets has not led to the more balanced movement of capital to all regions or to increasing the share of the least developed countries in trade. It has, rather, concentrated capital flows to the already developed and the fast-developing countries. In the early 1990s over two-thirds of total foreign direct investments to developing countries went to less than a dozen of them. These same countries accounted also for over two-thirds of total exports originating from developing countries. At the same time, we find a phenomenon where even in the more advanced economies minimum legal standards and social safety nets are proving more and more difficult to guarantee because of weakened control of governments over many aspects of economic life.

The ILO has been fully engaged in examining the social dimensions of globalization, especially under the aegis of the *Working Group on the Social Dimensions of Globalization and Liberalization of International Trade*. This book fills an important gap in these continuing discussions, which have not yet addressed the important question of how to provide for the expected rise in labor mobility in the twenty-first century. By alerting us to the future prospects for labor migration and the issues likely to be raised for the international community, this book, it is hoped, will help stimulate thinking into what should be the shape of a future migration regime that fully respects the rights of individual migrants, while enhancing the positive role of migration in growth and development.

Werner Sengenberger
Director
Employment Strategy Department
ILO

1

Globalization in Perspective

The farther and more deeply we penetrate into matter, by means of increasingly powerful methods, the more we are confounded by the interdependence of its parts . . . All around us, as far as the eye can see, the universe holds together, and only one way of considering it is really possible, that is, to take it as a whole, in one piece.

—*Pierre Teilhard de Chardin*[1]

Globalization has long been an alluring vision. Philosophers and politicians have often welcomed the prospect of a universal, peaceful unity. Certainly the world seems to be binding itself ever more tightly into seamless webs and networks. Computers are jetting from Malaysia to the United States, apples from Chile to Europe, and gold and wine are flowing from South Africa all over the world. At the same time, trillions of dollars are flashing out as electronic impulses daily from the world's major financial centers in London, New York, and Tokyo. Permeating all this traffic is a blizzard of cultural and commercial images that make thousands of personalities and brand names instantly recognizable the world over.

But all this has had surprisingly little to do with the movement of people. Discussions of globalization rarely consider international migration at all, or if they do they deal with it as a residual category, an afterthought. This could be a matter of relative scale. Trade and finance are moving in much more impressive quantities: in 1996 global exports of goods represented around 29 percent of world GDP, and the inflow of foreign direct investment accounted for around 6 percent of gross domestic investment.[2] Global labor migration, on the other hand, is more limited, involving only around 120 million people—equivalent to 2.3 percent of world population.[3]

Yet migration, or the fear of it, is closely connected with other aspects of globalization and is influencing many international debates.

The purpose of this book is to redress the balance somewhat, looking more closely at the movement of people—and seeing how they link up with other aspects of globalization.

What Is Globalization?

Such is the preoccupation with globalization that, whether welcomed or feared, it is being accepted as something new and startling—and out of human control. This is far from true. In many respects what we are currently going through is merely the latest, and not necessarily the most dramatic, phase of a centuries-long process. Far from being something remote and unmanageable, it is actually the outcome of deliberate choice. This is not to deny the significance of what is happening to the global economy, but it is important to be realistic about the scale and character of the changes.

A logical first task is to establish what "globalization" is—no simple matter since the term is applied to so many different processes that its meaning becomes steadily more elusive. In its weakest sense, it may merely refer to an increasing number of events taking place simultaneously in more than one country—from the emergence of soccer as a global sport to the resurgence of Islam as a global religion. But globalization should imply something beyond similarity or equivalence in each country—that these events are connected, and that there is a steady multiplication and intensification of links and flows between discrete national entities.

However, even this, strictly speaking, is only "internationalization." In its strongest sense, globalization goes beyond internationalization. It implies a higher plane of organization—one at which discrete national entities are themselves dissolving so that all major political and economic decisions will ultimately be transmitted globally. This new world sees the "death of geography" and in particular the demise of the nation-state.

In practice, the word is generally used more loosely. Almost all international processes are considered as aspects of globalization. Additionally, this umbrella term is subsuming many processes that are essentially national. It thus includes many aspects of economic liberalization, such as privatization, that are clearly under the control of national governments.

Mixed up with all this is a dash of ideological rhetoric. Globalization has embedded within the concept both a description and a prescription. The description is of a world ever more closely bound by flows of trade and finance. The prescription is that this is how the world ought to be—that such developments are in everyone's interest.

Globalization in History

Globalization in the sense of widespread international trade is usually regarded as a phenomenon of the past decade or so. This is strange, since the internationalization of commerce is scarcely novel. Private corporations have operated across national borders for at least five hundred years. In the Middle Ages in Europe, for example, numerous trading companies established offices and representatives in cities across the continent. The merchants of the German Hanseatic League, for example, had myriad interests: they helped develop agriculture in Poland, iron production in Sweden, and general industry in Belgium. In the fourteenth century, the Medici formed one of the first transnational banks—with trading and banking houses scattered throughout Europe. In later centuries, enterprises such as the East India Company and the Hudson's Bay Company extended the concept—expanding their operations along with the British Empire and becoming the progenitors of the modern transnational enterprise.[4]

The internationalization of business also owed a great deal to the Industrial Revolution. The industrializing countries looked overseas for raw materials and foodstuffs, and also for new markets for their output, and they invested heavily. By the outbreak of World War I, foreign direct investment had reached an estimated $14 billion.[5] The 1930s saw something of a lull, but transnational growth took off again after World War II, initially driven by American companies, but later also by those of Europe and Japan.

The historical growth in transnational investment was accompanied by a similar expansion of trade. Between 1870 and 1913, international trade expanded at around 3.4 percent per year. Between 1913 and 1950, there was then a long hiatus, as a result of wars and various types of trade restriction, during which growth plummeted to less than 1 percent annually. Then it recovered—between 1950 and 1973, trade grew at over 9 percent per year.[6]

Along with an internationalization of investment and trade there have also been significant movements of people. The most brutal transfers resulted from the slave trade. Prior to 1850, an estimated 15 million slaves were transported from Africa to the Americas, and during the century following the abolition of slavery, over 30 million people were moved as indentured workers.[7] However, millions more people would also travel voluntarily. Over the period 1846 to 1939, some 59 million people were to leave Europe, mostly heading for the Americas, but also for Australia, New Zealand, and South Africa.[8]

Capital in Perspective

One might assume that, as a result of this long history of transfers of goods and people, the world today is now more international than at any time in history. But this is questionable. Indeed it can be argued that the world was much more "globalized" during earlier periods. This is evident even when considering movements of capital. One 1980 study that measured financial openness in terms of the ratio of national current account balances to GDP found that a number of European and North American countries were no more open than they had been a century earlier. In fact, for six of the major countries (Great Britain, Italy, Sweden, Norway, Denmark, and the United States) there had been a relative decline in capital movements.[9]

Another aspect of global integration is the trading of currencies and securities—and the strength of links between one financial center and another. In recent years, there have been concerns about systemic collapses as a result of the ease with which currency traders can move funds around the world in response to economic weaknesses or changes in interest rates. However, a number of investigations have suggested that, in terms of the interlinking of global interest rates, the time of greatest correlation in short-term rates between different countries was actually during the period of the gold standard from 1879 to 1914.[10] Similar conclusions have been drawn about the extent of transnational securities trading—that markets were actually more integrated in the late nineteenth and early twentieth centuries than they are today.[11]

Trade in Perspective

Nor does trade seem to be much more significant now than in earlier periods. Figure 1.1 shows merchandise exports as a proportion of GDP. It shows that the percentage for Western Europe is consistently higher than for the United States. This is not surprising since smaller countries generally depend more on external trade than larger ones. Even so, by this criterion economies large or small seem to be little more open to trade than they were at the beginning of this century.

However, these aggregates say nothing about the composition of GDP—and this could help account for this apparent paradox. Nowadays many more people are employed in services, and particularly the public sector. This on its own would depress the ratio of trade to GDP and mask a rise in trade volume. Another factor will be the

Figure 1.1   Merchandise Exports as Percentage of GDP, 1890–1992

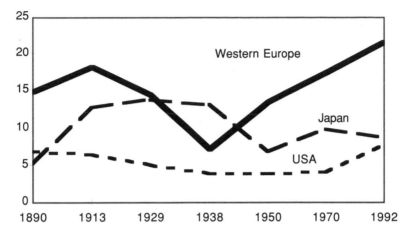

Source: Bairoch, P., 1996.
Note: Data are three-year averages, except 1950.

change in the composition of exports and particularly their prices. For the United States, at the beginning of the twentieth century, for example, less than one-third of trade was of manufactured goods rather than commodities, while today the proportion is around 75 percent.[12]

One of the most surprising elements of the above chart is the position of Japan, which, on this measure, is less trade-dependent than it was before World War II.[13] It should be pointed out again, however, that merchandise here is being measured in terms of prices. This will make its relative importance sensitive to a change in relative prices between exports and domestic consumption. Thus, while the volume of Japanese exports has risen, the prices of exports have fallen relative to domestic consumption. Nevertheless, even after taking these considerations into account, it does seem that economies are not dramatically more open nowadays than previously.

Migration in Perspective

One could add similar caveats about the international flows of people. While many people are concerned about the large numbers of international migrants, in fact historically the largest flows were in the century after 1815. This can be illustrated by the case of the largest receiving country, the United States. The number of immigrants today is considered high, but as Figure 1.2 shows, it is actually less than at the beginning of this century. Moreover, as a proportion of the recipient population it is even less significant. In 1914 (the peak year) the total number of immigrants was 1.2 million, which was 1.5 percent of the total American population, while in 1996 they came to 911,000, which was only 0.35 percent of the population.[14]

Recent global migration data based on national censuses are shown in Table 1.1. For most countries the data refer to the foreign-born population (who may subsequently have become citizens of their new country) and for most of the rest they refer to noncitizens. They also include refugees. As the table indicates, the total global migrant stock increased between 1965 and 1990 from 75 million to 120 million. This may seem a large increase—1.9 percent per year. But it is only slightly above the world's average of 1.8 percent population growth rate over the same period.[15]

A Global Consciousness

If the basic data suggest that the world is no more internationalized than it was at the beginning of this century, why is it that the world seems much more global? One reason may be that many indicators of globalization have been rising in the last few years. So the "inexorable"

Figure 1.2   U.S. Immigration, 1820–1998

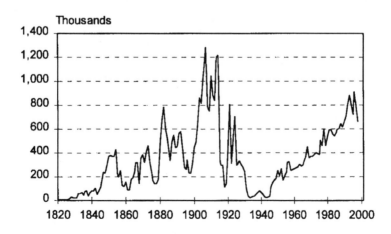

Source: U.S. Immigration and Naturalization Service, various years.

Table 1.1   World Migrant Stock by Region, 1965–1990

	Thousands				As % of total population			
	1965	1975	1985	1990	1965	1975	1985	1990
World	75,214	84,494	105,194	119,761	2.3	2.1	2.2	2.3
Industrial countries	30,401	38,317	47,991	54,231	3.1	3.5	4.1	4.5
Developing countries	44,813	46,177	57,203	65,530	1.9	1.6	1.6	1.6
Africa	7,952	11,178	12,527	15,631	2.5	2.7	2.3	2.5
Asia	31,429	29,662	38,731	43,018	1.7	1.3	1.4	1.4
L. America/Caribbean	5,907	5,788	6,410	7,475	2.4	1.8	1.6	1.7
Northern America	12,695	15,042	20,460	23,895	6.0	6.3	7.8	8.6
Europe/former USSR	14,728	19,504	22,959	25,068	2.2	2.7	3.0	3.2
Oceania	2,502	3,319	4,106	4,675	14.4	15.6	16.9	17.8

Source: Zlotnik, H., 1998.

process of globalization may be based on extrapolations of recent trends that historically have shown themselves capable of reversal.

But it can also be argued that international flows have not just been increasing in volume, but have also been changing in character. This can be seen, for example, in the much deeper integration achieved by transnational corporations, which can disperse production of parts across many different production sites—a process helped by the speed of communications and the cheapness of transportation. By 1990, for example, air transport costs per mile were less than 20 percent of their 1930 level,[16] and between 1930 and 1996 the cost of a three-minute telephone conversation between London and New York fell from $300 to $1.[17]

The character of international migration has also changed. Migrants can move back and forth much more readily and rapidly—and can keep in regular contact with their homes, even if these are on the other side of the globe. As a result, the flows are more diverse and complex. The International Labour Organization (ILO) has looked at current patterns for 152 countries, considering their proportions of immigrants and emigrants, as well as the volumes of remittances. It finds that, between 1970 and 1990, the number of countries that qualified as major receivers went up from thirty-nine to sixty-seven and those that qualified as major senders went up from twenty-nine to fifty-five. But one of the most interesting conclusions was the increase in the number of countries that were both major senders and receivers—up from four to fifteen.[18]

These developments have also affected the way we see the world. As a leading sociologist commentator on globalization has expressed it: "Globalization refers both to the compression of the world and the intensification of consciousness of the world as a whole."[19] Again it could be argued that even this is nothing new. Many "universal" theoretical frameworks have been applied to international relations, from Marxist analysis of global capitalism to more recent presentations in terms of "world-systems theory." But these have essentially referred to relationships between states, economies, or cultures—that is, between relatively independent entities.[20] The essence of globalization is that barriers between these entities are dissolving—and opening up the possibility of some kind of global consciousness.

The Modern Era

Where has this consciousness come from? What seems like the fusion of different systems may merely be an extension of the process of modernization. The latest communications technologies, for example, are another step in the development of calendars and mapping. These were the basis of establishing the universal date and time zones that allow for extensive coordination and synchronization. Time and space have thus become objects to be manipulated. Many other aspects of life have been "codified" to make them uniform and exchangeable—in particular the universal media of financial exchange, from cash to credit cards.

Some would argue, however, that the emergence of a global consciousness is less the integration of the remotest parts of the world into one single reflexive organism and more the spread and domination of one particular way of life—liberal capitalism and the technology it has developed. Rather than integrating many systems into one large synthesis, modernism seems to be sweeping everything else aside in favor of one pervasive and uniform system.

This probably gives too much weight to the efficacy of "cultural imperialism" and underestimates the resilience of many other cultures and their ability to resist deep penetration and to continually transform themselves on their own terms. The most deliberate high-profile opposition has appeared in the form of Islamic fundamentalism, which has at times resisted both democracy and modernization. But many of the emerging Asian countries are also very selective about the aspects of Western culture they wish to take on board. They have made rapid progress, they say, because of the strength of their own values; not because they became like the West, but because they have remained different from the West.[21] The Asian financial crisis added several question marks to this assumption, however, with the suggestion that such family network–based value systems may have contributed to the collapse.[22]

The Retreat of the State

Throughout history, the commercial aspects of globalization have also been intimately connected with the rise—and fall—of the nation-state. Initially the emergence of the nation-state relied very much on modern media and uniform systems of education that helped create and sustain national identity and state power. Now, however, it seems that the modern era of globalization is eroding the authority of the state and the significance of national borders.

This erosion is a matter of deliberate choice. Governments, the guardians of national identity, have been retreating from areas previously considered their exclusive prerogative—removing many forms of welfare protection and services and passing to the private sector many activities previously the domain of state-owned corporations. But at the same time they have been making decisions that have reduced the significance of national borders—notably promoting free trade and removing restrictions on international movements of capital.

The retreat of the state has opened up much more room for private enterprise at national and international levels. This process has, of course, been accelerated by the collapse of communism and a further spread of the principles of liberal democracy. But in practice most governments, whatever ideology they profess, are moving roughly in the same direction. States are therefore deliberately choosing to reduce their own significance. This has profound implications for global governance and regulation, since at present the global institutions that might take over some of the functions ceded by national governments remain relatively weak.

However, one should not assume that every change has global implications. In many cases, what has been happening has been more a process of regionalization—as countries, and parts of countries, realign themselves according to the logic of production and markets rather than of national borders. Some of these regions may actually lie within national borders, such as northern Italy, Pusan at the southern tip of the Korean Peninsula, or the Shukoten region of Japan (whose GNP would rank it third worldwide after the United States and Germany). But many others straddle national borders, such as the Growth Triangle that consists of Singapore, Johore (a state in Malaysia), and the Riau Islands of Indonesia. They are uniting because they form natural economic zones.[23]

These political developments have again been amplified by dramatic developments in technology—notably the spread of digital communications. Even the most repressive regime can be undermined by an unstoppable flow of information and criticism. But governments are also faced with many new forms of production and wealth that glide around cyberspace beyond most forms of control—or taxation.

Conclusion

Globalization is more realistically viewed as the latest phase in a long historical process—and in some respects not the most significant. An analysis by sociologist Roland Robertson divides globalization into a number of broad periods. Currently, he says, we are moving through the "Era of Uncertainty."[24]

Globalization is not a monolithic, unstoppable juggernaut, but rather a complex web of interrelated processes—some of which are subject to greater control than others. Of these, international migration is the one most likely to provoke intervention. Governments are less willing nowadays to block flows of trade or finance but take much more resolute action when it comes to people.

But why should they need to do this? In theory, globalization should eventually make countries economically more equivalent so people should not need to move around the world searching for work. The next chapter looks at the prospects for this kind of "convergence."

Notes

1. Teilhard de Chardin, P. 1955, p. 48.
2. World Bank, 1998b.
3. Zlotnik, H. 1998.
4. Dunning, J. 1993, p. 97.
5. Ibid., p. 116.
6. Hirst, P., and G. Thompson. 1996, p. 21.
7. Appleyard, R. 1991, p. 11.
8. Stalker, P. 1994, p. 74.
9. Grassman, S. 1980, p. 51.
10. Hirst, P., and G. Thompson. 1996, p. 35.
11. Ibid.
12. Bairoch, P. 1996, p. 180.
13. Ibid., p. 179.
14. U.S. Immigration and Naturalization Service. 1996.
15. Zlotnik, H. 1998, p. 1.
16. World Bank. 1995, p. 51.
17. *Economist,* 1997.
18. Böhning, W., and N. Oishi. 1995, p. 794.
19. Robertson, R. 1992, p. 8.
20. Waters, M. 1996, p. 25.
21. Huntingdon, S. 1996, p. 38.
22. *Economist,* 1998b.
23. Ohmae, K. 1996, p. 80.
24. Robertson, R. 1992.

2

Convergence and Divergence

According to neoclassical economic theory, one effect of globalization should be "factor price equalization." Goods, people, and capital moving across national borders should tend to equalize prices between countries. Labor should travel from low-wage to high-wage economies and capital should move in the other direction. This would tend to depress wages in the migrant-destination countries, while raising them in the sending countries. Eventually, some kind of equilibrium should be reached when the remaining wage gap represents just the cost of migration between the two countries. As a result, migration should stop.

Does this equalization happen in practice? This is difficult to judge at present. Although capital and goods can move fairly freely, labor cannot. Today, all states exert, or try to exert, very strict control over their borders and want to avoid any mass influx of new people.

In the past things were very different: for centuries people were free to move as they wished without passports or visas. To assess the effect of migration on international wages, therefore, it is easier to inspect the historical record. Economic historian Jeffrey Williamson has done this by examining data over the past 150 years for fifteen countries. In the New World, these countries were Australia, Argentina, Canada, and the United States. In the Old World they were Belgium, Denmark, France, Germany, Great Britain, Ireland, Italy, the Netherlands, Norway, Spain, and Sweden.

The First Era of Convergence—Europe Catches Up

These data point to two distinct eras of convergence. The first covers the period 1870–1913, and the process of convergence is illustrated in Figure 2.1. This indicates changes in urban unskilled wage rates adjusted for the local cost of living. The extent to which wages differ across countries is expressed by a "coefficient of dispersion." Further, as Figure 2.1 indicates, from 1870 to around 1900 the trend is a steady process of convergence, with the coefficient almost halved—from 0.24 to 0.14.

Most of the convergence represents European wages catching up with those in the Americas, and wages in Argentina and Canada in the process of catching up with Australia and the United States. Even so, the United States remained comfortably ahead of most other countries—in 1900, real wages in the United States were still 62 percent higher than in Great Britain. There had also been considerable convergence between the countries of northern Europe. In Sweden in 1854, real wages were only 48 percent of those in Great Britain, but by 1913 they were at a par. Ireland too made significant progress over the same period—the ratio rising from 60 to 92 percent. However, there remained a persistent wage gap in Europe between the richer countries of the north and the poorer countries of the south.

What led to this convergence? The fact that it took place in a relatively open period suggests that globalization played an important part. This was an era of free trade and currencies were linked through the gold standard. Migration was relatively free—between 1846 and 1924 an estimated 50 million Europeans migrated to the traditional receiving countries of North America and Australia.[1]

Williamson concludes that the main factors were trade and migration. The trade component was largely the result of rapidly falling transport costs between North America and Europe. This dramatically

Figure 2.1   International Real Wage Rate Dispersion, 1870–1913

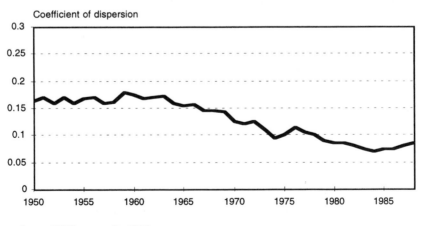

Source: Williamson, J., 1995.

lowered commodity prices in Europe. Thus the price of grain in Liverpool, which in 1870 was 60 percent higher than in Chicago, was only 15 percent higher by 1912—and there was also substantial price convergence in most other commodities, from beef, to coal, to copper. As a result, the cost of living in European countries fell, and real wages rose. Looking specifically at the gap between Great Britain and the United States, Williamson concludes that, in the years 1870–1895, commodity price convergence was responsible for more than one-third of the fall in the real wage gap between the two countries.[2]

The second factor he identifies is mass migration. Following the neoclassical model of factor-price equalization, this should have depressed real wages in the United States and raised them in Europe. However, the effect of immigration on wages is complex, for while the arrival of immigrants certainly increases the size of the labor force, it also creates more employment. For one thing, immigrants increase demand: they are consumers who will need, among other things, extra housing, food, and infrastructure whose provision will itself create more jobs. For another, they also offer a fresh and vigorous labor pool that itself attracts new capital that then expands employment. This clearly happened during this period. Capital was chasing labor: in the nineteenth century, most capital flows were from the Old World to the New, seeking opportunities for profit in the Americas.

So immigration might be expected to depress wages. But not necessarily. Indeed, some contemporary studies argued that immigration could not have retarded wage growth over this period since during the 1880s real wages in the United States actually rose. Other investigators, however, who compared wage growth during the immigration period with that during the migration-restricted 1920s, suggested that although real wages had not fallen in the earlier period, they had certainly grown more slowly. Williamson concurs. Using a computable general equilibrium model, he finds that migration did have a dampening effect on wages. Even allowing for capital movement, he concludes that without mass immigration, urban real wages in 1910 would have been more than 9 percent higher.[3]

Meanwhile wages should correspondingly have been rising in the sending countries. With emigration siphoning off excess labor, the demand for workers ought to have been increasing. In a number of countries, this emigration involved a substantial proportion of the population. Between 1846 and 1924, 22 percent of the population of Sweden, for example, and 41 percent of the population of the British Isles had emigrated. Indeed, on average, emigrants from Europe over this period represented 12.3 percent of the population.[4] Emigration on this scale must have had an impact on wages, and there were in fact substantial wage rises in Sweden and Ireland.

Of course there are other reasons apart from emigration why real wages might have risen. One is new technology: the diffusion of technology from the more advanced to the less advanced countries would have helped increase their productivity, as would rising standards of education. However, in the late nineteenth century most industrial technologies were well known, and already available around the globe, and did not require a particularly educated work force. Williamson's overall conclusion is that around 70 percent of real wage convergence between 1870 and 1910 was due to mass migration, leaving the rest due to other forces such as trade.

World War I brought this period of convergence to a halt, not just in trade and investment, but also in migration. Before the war, there had been relatively few restrictions on international travel. People were free to move throughout Europe—and sometimes overseas—without passports, and if they wanted to settle in a new country there were few bureaucratic obstacles. However, restrictions had steadily been building up, particularly in the United States, and after the war immigration became very difficult: arrivals that had been running at over a million per year were cut to around 162,000.[5] This process of "deglobalization" was accompanied by a divergence in real wage rates. The dispersion coefficient started to rise again and, by the end of World War II, was still as high as 2.0.

The Second Era of Convergence— Barriers Fall in Europe

The second major period of convergence took place from the beginning of the 1960s, as indicated in Figure 2.2. This has two main components. The first consists of Europe catching up with the New World. In 1960, real wages in West Germany, for example, were only 39 percent of those in the United States, while by 1988 they were up to 89 percent. Similarly, in Denmark the ratio rose from 54 percent to 100 percent. At the same time, there was also considerable convergence within Europe as Italy, Spain, and France caught up with many of the countries of Northern Europe.[6]

What had caused convergence during the second period? Conditions were certainly very different. Migration from Europe to North America had been considerably reduced. In the decade 1901–1910, more than 8 million Europeans had left for North America, but by the decade 1961–1970 the flow had fallen to 1.1 million, and by 1981–1990 to 0.8 million. For some countries the falls were dramatic, and continued through the period of convergence. Thus departures

Figure 2.2   International Real Wage Dispersion, 1946–1988

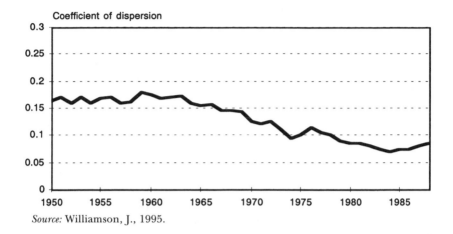

Source: Williamson, J., 1995.

from the Federal Republic of Germany during 1951–1960 were more than half a million, but by 1981–1990 had fallen to 91,000.[7]

Convergence thus had little to do with emigration. Instead it was more a result of economic growth in Europe. In the countries of the European Community, per capita GDP in the 1960s was rising on average by 4.8 percent per year, compared with 3.0 percent in North America, and although growth slowed in subsequent decades, it was still faster in Europe than in North America. The same period also saw convergence in wages. Between 1970 and 1991, real wages grew by over 50 percent in the European Community (EC) compared with only 10 percent in the United States—though this was offset to some extent by a rise in unemployment.[8]

While Europe as a whole had been catching up, there had also been considerable convergence within Europe—particularly between countries of the European Community where cross-border investment and trade were helping to reduce disparities. Between 1960 and 1992, trade between the founder states increased from 35 to 60 percent of all their trade. This growth in trade brought a much greater degree of economic convergence. In addition, the EC had various regional and other funds that helped iron out imbalances.[9]

These developments also affected flows of migrants between European countries. In the 1950s, the poorer countries of the south, notably Spain, Portugal, and Italy, had dispatched large numbers of workers to the richer countries such as France and the Federal Republic of Germany. But as economic growth proceeded, and all countries became richer, so intra-European migration slowed—even though it was much easier for nationals of the various member states of the EC to work in other member countries. This was something of a relief. In the 1960s, there had been fears of an Italian "flood" to the richer countries. Instead, more Italians started to stay at home. During the period 1966–1970 Italy had a net loss of over 250,000 people, but by 1976–1980 the flows had started to reverse.[10]

In fact, Europe as a whole had become a net importer of labor, attracting workers from North Africa, Eastern Europe, and Turkey. As a result, countries such as Italy and Spain that had been exporters of labor now found themselves net importers. Figure 2.3 illustrates this process for Spain. From 1969 to 1973, emigration was over 100,000 per year, but from 1974 onwards it fell dramatically, stabilizing at around 20,000 per year.[11] The estimate of foreigners resident here does not take account of undocumented residents whose numbers in the early 1990s have been estimated at around 300,000.[12]

The evidence for Organisation for Economic Co-operation and Development (OECD) countries suggests, therefore, that movements of all factors of production contributed to convergence, but the relative contributions varied in different periods. In the first period, one of the major factors was mass migration that, together with commodity trading, helped even out real wage imbalances. In the second period, convergence was more a consequence of investment, trade,

Figure 2.3   Spain, Emigration, and Foreign Residents, 1960–1990

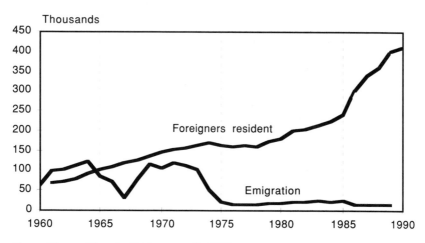

Source: Blanco Fdez. de Valderrama, C., 1993.

and economic development that served to reduce the incentives for migration between OECD countries.

Divergence Between OECD Countries and the Rest of the World

Almost all the above evidence on convergence refers to industrial countries. When it comes to the world as a whole, the picture is very different. Here, there seems to have been considerable divergence between the richest and poorest countries. A World Bank study estimated the extent of this divergence using purchasing power parity in 1985 dollars. It concluded that, between 1870 and 1960, the per capita income of the richest country (the United States) rose from $2,181 to $16,779. Meanwhile over the same period, the income of the poorest countries, such as Ethiopia, only rose from $250 to $325. As a result, the ratio between the two increased from around 9:1 to over 50:1. This divergence has continued. Between 1960 and 1990, income in the OECD countries grew on average by 2.6 percent per year, but in other countries it grew only by 1.8 percent. Over these three decades, the ratio of the incomes of the richest to the poorest countries rose by 45 percent.[13]

The United Nations Development Programme (UNDP) has arrived at similar conclusions, though it divides the world up differently. The 1996 *Human Development Report* estimated that, between 1960 and 1991, the share of global income of the richest 20 percent of the world's people rose from 70 to 85 percent while that of the poorest declined from 2.3 to 1.4 percent. By 1993, of the $23 trillion of global GDP, $18 trillion was in industrial countries and only $5 trillion in developing countries.[14]

If developing countries are to narrow the gap they will need much higher growth rates. Unfortunately, even during the healthier period of growth in the 1960s, average annual per capita growth in real GDP for the developing countries as a whole was only 3.3 percent. In the 1970s, this fell to 3.1 percent and in the 1980s to 1.2 percent. There were notable exceptions. Growth in East Asia averaged 6.3 percent in the 1980s. But given their low starting position and unimpressive growth rates, the developing countries as a whole were falling even further behind.[15]

Why have OECD countries been converging between themselves, while diverging with the rest of the world? This is partly a reflection of the fairly narrow base of "globalization." In fact the majority of world investment and trade takes place between industrial countries.

Of the total global stock of $1.9 trillion of foreign direct investment in 1992, just $420 billion (22 percent) was in developing countries.[16] There was a similar concentration in flows of trade—with most world exports coming from Europe, North America, and Japan.

While developing countries were only weakly integrated into the global economy, the centrally planned economies of Eastern Europe and the Soviet Union had even less contact. In the early years, this did not seem much of a disadvantage. Back in the 1930s, the Soviet Union had avoided the slump; indeed it had grown faster than every other country apart from Japan. Up to about 1960, the economies of the socialist countries as a whole grew much faster than those of the West, due largely to an expansion of heavy industry.[17] But during the 1960s and 1970s, the centrally planned economies started to lag behind the consumer-driven economies of the West.

Even so, there was still relatively little poverty. Before economic reforms started in 1990, there was virtually zero unemployment and very low levels of absolute poverty. This degree of equity had, however, been achieved at the cost of economic efficiency—as state-owned enterprises hoarded large numbers of underemployed workers. The reforms—and the opening up to the West—had been designed to increase efficiency and output, even at the expense of equity. Instead, there was a drastic fall in output—over 10 percent per year.

Conclusion

Countries can converge economically for a number of reasons—as a result of the flow of goods, or capital, or people. In the past the flow of people did help economies move closer together. But in recent years political resistance to migration has stifled this process—and contributed to a widening of international disparities. This has not stopped migration but it has has changed the pattern and direction of flows. The next chapter looks at the current disparities in earning potential that provoke migration between poor and rich countries.

Notes

1. Appleyard, R. 1991, p. 11.
2. Williamson, J. 1996, p. 286.
3. Ibid., p. 291.
4. Massey, D. 1988, p. 386.
5. Hatton, T., and J. Williamson. 1998, p. 247.
6. Williamson, J. 1995, p. 161.

7. U.S. Immigration and Naturalization Service. 1996.
8. OECD. 1994, p. 60.
9. Salt, J. 1996, p. 77.
10. Federici, N. 1989, p. 59.
11. Blanco Fdez. de Valderrama, C. 1993, p. 169.
12. Huntoon, L. 1998, p. 432.
13. Pritchett, L. 1996, p. 40.
14. UNDP. 1996, p. 12.
15. ILO. 1995, p. 29.
16. Ibid., p. 43.
17. Hobsbawm, E. 1994, p. 377.

3

The New Age of Migration

Divergence between the richer economies of the West and those of many developing countries has produced tempting disparities in wages—and is prompting many new kinds of migration flow. While many people migrate to other countries to advance their careers, or just out of a sense of adventure, for most people the main reason is the prospect of earning more money.

International Wage Disparities

The crudest way of assessing the difference in earnings potential between countries is in terms of average income per capita. On this measure, the border between the United States and Mexico is one of the longest between two countries with sharp income differentials: in terms of GDP per capita, the ratio between the two is 6:1. However, the steepest long cross-border differential is probably between Germany and Poland. Germany's per capita GDP is much the same as that of the United States, but Poland is so much poorer than Mexico that the income ratio across the border is 11:1.

The average GDP says nothing about how income is distributed in either country—or about wage levels. A more realistic picture of the potential for migration is the difference in wage rates for occupations that are open to immigrants. These contrasts may be greater or smaller.

- *Mexico–United States*—A survey was carried out in 1996 of 465 Mexicans who had been apprehended and removed from the United States. They reported that they earned an average $31 per week in their last Mexican job compared with $278 per week in the United States, which would make the ratio 9:1.[1]

21

- *Poland-Germany*—Hourly wages for Polish construction workers in Germany in 1996 were around DM7 compared with DM2 they might earn in Poland.[2]
- *Indonesia-Malaysia*—In 1997, Indonesian laborers could earn $0.28 a day at home compared with $2 or more in neighboring Malaysia.[3]

A broader range of comparisons is illustrated in Table 3.1, which shows hourly wage costs in manufacturing around the world. Apart from showing the sharp differences in wages between industrial and developing countries, this also shows how wages in countries like the Republic of Korea and Singapore increased dramatically, making them magnets for their poorer neighbors.[4]

However, the decision to migrate will not be determined entirely by wage differentials. Migrants will also have to consider issues such as the likelihood of finding work in the new country, the chances of being deported if they are entering illegally, and the costs of migration, both financial and psychological. This can be formulated as an identity that expresses the "net return to migration" (Box 3.1).[5]

Where there is a free and rapid exchange of information across national borders, as between Mexico and the United States, migrant flows can be very sensitive to changes in relative wage rates. A study in the United States by the Public Policy Institute examined the flows of undocumented immigrants to California from Mexico between 1980 and 1993. It found that when California's economy boomed in the mid to late 1980s, the state experienced brisk job growth and undocumented immigration peaked. On the other hand, when California suffered from a severe recession in the early 1990s, undocumented immigration fell.[6] Migrants do generally know where the jobs are and the prospects of finding one. A 1998 review of Mexico-U.S. migration concluded that 95 percent of Mexicans who come to look for a job do find one—and it takes them on average only about one month to do so.[7]

Migration decisions are also affected by conditions in the sending country: when the Mexican economy is in crisis, undocumented migration rises. One study has concluded that a 10 percent decrease in real wages in Mexico is associated with an 8 percent increase in apprehensions of undocumented immigrants at the border.[8]

At first glance, the model in Box 3.1 suggests that the highest migration rates should be from the poorest countries to the richest. This has not been the case in the past. In the nineteenth century, intercontinental migrations actually started from the wealthier sending countries—first England, and subsequently Germany. The poorer countries of southern Europe only sent people later. Indeed, historically there is

Table 3.1   Hourly Labor Costs in Manufacturing (U.S.$), 1980–1995

	1980	1985	1995
United States	9.87	13.01	17.20
Canada	8.67	10.94	16.03
Australia	8.47	8.20	14.40
New Zealand	5.33	4.47	10.11
Europe			
France	8.94	5.72	19.34
Germany	12.33	9.60	31.88
Italy	8.15	7.63	16.48
United Kingdom	7.56	6.27	13.77
Austria	8.88	7.58	25.33
Belgium	13.11	8.97	26.88
Denmark	10.83	8.13	24.19
Finland	8.24	8.16	24.78
Netherlands	12.06	8.75	24.18
Norway	11.59	10.37	24.38
Spain	5.89	4.66	12.70
Sweden	12.51	9.66	21.36
Switzerland	11.09	9.66	29.28
Czech Republic	n.a.	n.a.	1.30
Hungary	n.a.	n.a.	1.70
Poland	n.a.	n.a.	2.09
Russian Federation	n.a.	n.a.	0.60
Asia			
Japan	5.52	6.34	23.66
Singapore	1.49	2.47	7.28
Hong Kong (China)	1.51	1.73	4.82
China	0.25	0.19	0.25
Taiwan (China)	1.00	1.50	5.82
Rep. of Korea	0.96	1.23	7.40
Malaysia	0.73	1.08	1.59
Thailand	0.31	0.49	0.46
Philippines	0.53	0.64	0.71
Indonesia	0.16	0.22	0.30
India	0.44	0.35	0.25

Source: Morgan Stanley and Co. Inc., 1996.

a fairly high correlation between the onset of large-scale emigration and the beginning of industrialization.[9]

Why should this be so? Some researchers point to the importance of personal wealth—which generally increases after industrialization starts. The very poorest, struggling to cover subsistence needs, may wish to migrate but are unlikely to have the money to travel internationally. With a little increase in income, however, families will be able to save or borrow the initial cost of sending someone overseas. In the Philippines, for example, more than 90 percent of departing contract

> ### Box 3.1   Calculating the Net Return to Migration
>
> The decisionmaking process for a potential migrant deciding whether to leave home can be expressed in the following identity:
>
> $$ER(0) = \int_{0}^{n} [P_1(t) P_2(t) Y_d(t) - P_3(t) Y_o(t)] e^{-n} dt - C(0), \text{ where}$$
>
> $ER(0)$ = Expected net return to migration calculated at time 0.
> t = time.
> $P_1(t)$ = Probability of avoiding deportation (from 0 to 1).
> $P_2(t)$ = Probability of employment at destination.
> $Y_d(t)$ = Earnings if employed at destination.
> $P_3(t)$ = Probability of employment at community of origin.
> r = Discount factor to reflect the greater utility of present money.
> $C(0)$ = Total costs of movement (financial and psychological).
>
> If $ER(0)$ is positive, the rational actor will migrate.
>
> On the basis of this identity, governments who wished to influence migration would attempt to affect earnings, the comparative probabilities of employment, and the costs of migration.
>
> *Source:* Massey, D., et al. 1993.

workers have been found to be employed before going overseas.[10] As incomes rise further, however, the need for migration decreases and the economic and social costs of migration rise, making it more attractive to stay at home. That it is not the poorest who emigrate is evident even in the case of migration from Puerto Rico to the United States, on which there are no restrictions. Very few Puerto Ricans with limited schooling migrate to the United States, perhaps because they lack language skills or information about jobs.[11]

A further implication of this model is that migration should decline as wage differentials between receiving and sending countries narrow. But this too is uncertain. Much will depend on the employment situation. Even if wages fall in the richer country, there could still be a greater likelihood of finding a job there, so migration could continue to increase.[12]

One aspect of economically driven migration that this model does not fully express is the migrant's judgment on long-term earnings. It is quite possible, for example, that individuals might choose to move to a country where they would initially earn less but where

Figure 3.1   Decision to Migrate Based on Long-Term Earnings

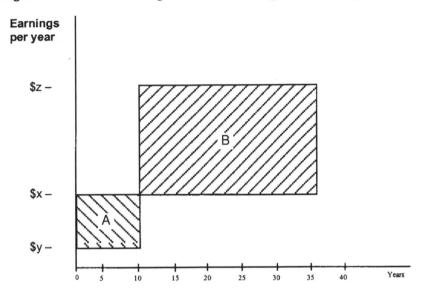

Source: Martin, P., and E. Midgley, 1994.

they believe they will gain in the long term. Philip Martin has illustrated this in the diagram adapted in Figure 3.1. He points to the possibility of an Irish lawyer or a Polish doctor who might be earning $30,000 per year at home. If they moved to the United States they might earn less because lawyers and doctors cannot work in their professions until they are certified. In the meantime they might have to deliver pizzas or drive a cab. The scenario in this diagram has a migrant who is earning $x per year at home, drops to $y per year for ten years in the United States, but eventually earns $z per year. Migration will be financially worthwhile if rectangle B is larger than rectangle A—which is more likely for a younger migrant with a longer working life ahead.

Another way of looking at this subject is to consider how low the ratio of incomes between sending and receiving countries has to be in order to halt immigration. Based on experience between the richer and poorer countries of Europe, it would seem that wage and job opportunity ratios do not have to be 1:1 (equal in the origin and destination areas) to stop labor migration. After wage ratios between the richer northern countries like France and Germany and the poorer countries of the south fell to around 4:1, relatively few people thought it worthwhile to migrate.[13]

Modern Migration Patterns

This large—and widening—gap between the industrial countries on one side, and the former socialist countries and the poorer developing countries on the other, along with political and other processes of globalization, has helped reshape international migration in the 1970s and 1980s. But these migration patterns are also linked with many other economic and social developments that influence migration flows. Some of the potential advantages and disadvantages are presented schematically in Table 3.2.

Traditional Receiving Countries

Flows into the largest receiving countries—the United States, Canada, Australia—that previously were dominated by Europeans are now overwhelmingly originating in the developing countries. These new patterns were largely the result of political changes. In the United States until the 1960s, national immigration quotas for countries outside the Western Hemisphere were set according to the actual immigration flows of the 1920s (when immigrants had come predominantly from Europe). However, the mood of civil rights sweeping the country in the 1960s was opposed to the implicitly racist basis of such controls, and first the Kennedy and then the Johnson administration changed the system with the 1965 Immigration and Nationality Act to give greater preference to those who already had relatives in the country. At the time it was presumed that this would cause few changes (since there were so many people with European ancestry), but in fact Asians and Latin Americans were to take up the option in much greater numbers.[14] As a result of this and other legislative changes, between 1951–1960 and 1981–1990, the proportion of immigrants coming from developing countries rose from 12 to 88 percent. Table 3.3 shows the sources of immigration to the United States for 1997.[15] In addition to these, there are large flows of undocumented arrivals: in 1996, there were an estimated 5 million undocumented immigrants—more than half of whom were from Mexico (Table 3.4).

Canada, too, made important changes to immigration policy in the 1960s. Previously, the system had shown a strong preference for white immigrants. Asians and blacks were not welcomed; indeed, they had at times been systematically excluded. Following legislative changes in 1962 and 1967, however, the system was overhauled to remove such discrimination and was based instead on the needs of the Canadian labor market. As Figure 3.2 illustrates, this had a dramatic effect on the ethnic origins of immigrants.[16] Australia made similar changes; until 1965 the country had a "white Australia" policy. Abolition of this policy also caused a radical shift. In the period 1959–1965,

Table 3.2 Advantages and Disadvantages of Migration

	Emigration from Sending Country		Immigration to Receiving Country	
	Potential Advantages	Potential Disadvantages	Potential Advantages	Potential Disadvantages
For migrants, or for individuals in receiving country	Employment Greater income Training or education New cultural experiences Meeting new people	Bad working conditions Long hours Lower status work Racism or discrimination Separation from family	Services that free women to enter labor force Cheaper goods and services Opportunities to move up to supervisory jobs Richer cultural life Learning about other countries	Competition for jobs Lower local wages Strange languages and customs Creation of immigrant ghettos
For enterprises	Skills of returning migrants Extra business for communications and travel firms	Losing skilled work force Labor shortages that drive up wages	Meeting labor shortages Cheaper, more flexible labor Larger markets and economies of scale	Need to give language or other training Dependence on foreign labor for certain jobs
For society	Lower unemployment Knowledge and skills of returnees Building transnational communities Foreign currency remittances Reduced population pressure	Coping with sudden returnees Brain drain and loss of better workers Culture of emigration Increasing inequality Losing younger people	Lower inflation Gaining people already educated More diverse and energetic population Capital brought by immigrant investors Tax income from younger workers Rejuvenating population	Slowing technological innovation Costs of language and other training Social friction Loss in balance of payments from remittances Cost of social services

Table 3.3   Sources of Legal Immigration to the United States, 1997

Country	1997 Arrivals	%
1. Mexico	163,572	18.4
2. Philippines	55,876	6.2
3. China	41,728	5.2
4. Viet Nam	42,067	4.8
5. India	44,859	4.8
6. Cuba	26,466	4.2
7. Dominican Republic	39,604	3.4
8. El Salvador	17,903	2.3
9. Jamaica	19,089	2.2
10. Russian Federation	19,668	2.1

Source: U.S. Immigration and Naturalization Service, 1997.

Table 3.4   Sources of Undocumented Immigrants in the United States, 1996

Country	1996 Stock	%
1. Mexico	2,700,000	54.0
2. El Salvador	335,000	5.6
3. Guatemala	165,000	3.3
4. Canada	120,000	2.4
5. Haiti	105,000	2.1
6. Philippines	95,000	1.9
7. Honduras	90,000	1.8
8. Poland	70,000	1.4
9. Nicaragua	70,000	1.4
10. Bahamas	70,000	1.4

Source: U.S. Immigration and Naturalization Service, 1998.

just 3 percent of settler arrivals were from Asia, but by 1994–1995 this had risen to 37 percent.[17]

Western Europe

Migration into Europe, from the 1950s onward, was in many cases initiated as a result of labor shortages. In the United Kingdom, for example, the flows of West Indians until 1961 showed a close correlation with the number of unfilled vacancies.[18] France too found itself short of workers and the government took the lead in foreign recruitment. In the 1950s, it encouraged the arrival (for long-term settlement) of workers from the Catholic countries of southern Europe; then, when these supplies were exhausted, it filled vacancies with Muslims from North Africa. In the 1960s, West Germany followed France's lead— concerned that the economy would not be able to sustain a high rate of growth at full employment without inflation. The Federal Republic

Figure 3.2   Canada, Sources of Immigrants, 1901–1990

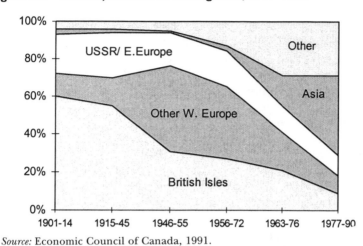

Source: Economic Council of Canada, 1991.

of Germany set up recruitment offices in the major sending countries—Italy, Greece, Turkey, and Yugoslavia—initially looking for seasonal workers and then *Gastarbeiter* to work on short-term contracts.[19] By 1973, France and the Federal Republic of Germany each had about 2.5 million foreign workers—accounting for 10–12 percent of their labor forces.[20] After the first oil shock in 1973, however, the demand for immigrants fell and European governments started to apply restrictions. But the tap, once turned on, proved difficult to turn off. Many of those who had arrived as temporary guest workers decided to stay—and brought their families to join them—and millions of others settled illegally. Germany in particular was to prove a magnet in subsequent years following the collapse of communism. Taking both parts of Germany together, over the period 1988–1994 net immigration to Germany totaled 4 million, due to the arrival of ethnic Germans, asylum seekers, new labor immigrants, and family members of previous immigrants.[21]

The Persian Gulf States

The hike in oil prices was a blow to immigrants heading for Europe, but it opened fresh opportunities in the Persian Gulf states. While there had always been traditional migratory movements between Arab states, the oil price rises triggered an explosion in the demand for labor, particularly for construction. At first, the gulf states met this demand by drawing in more workers from neighboring countries, but they soon had to look further afield, particularly to Asia. Between 1975 and 1990, the number of immigrant workers in the seven members of the Gulf Cooperation Council had increased from 1.1 million to 5.2 million and made up 68 percent of the labor force.[22] Immigration continued after oil prices started to decline in the period 1985–1990, though rather more slowly, with more workers arriving for the service industries than for construction. The Gulf War of 1990–1991 was a traumatic time for immigrant workers and millions had to leave. Gradually many returned, and although governments have declared that they do not wish to rely so much on foreign labor, they seem to be as dependent as ever. In Kuwait in 1996, of a total labor force of 1.1 million, only 176,000 were Kuwaiti citizens.[23]

East and Southeast Asia

While countries in Europe and the Persian Gulf were turning to migrant workers to meet their labor needs, a similar situation was developing further east. Japan's remarkable postwar transformation had been achieved with few foreign workers. This was primarily because Japan had been a relatively closed country concerned about the social impact that immigrants might have in a relatively homogenous society.[24] So rather than meet labor gaps with immigrants, Japan increased levels of technology to reduce the labor content of manufacturing, and also invested heavily in production overseas. But this was only a partial solution and during the late 1980s shortages became very acute.

Many of these vacancies were filled by immigrants on short-term contracts, so that by 1995 the number of foreign residents registered in Japan reached a record high of 1.36 million.[25] This represented nearly 1.1 percent of the population—though around half of these people were Koreans, many of whom had been in Japan for generations. In addition, there have also been large numbers of undocumented arrivals—generally people entering as tourists and overstaying their visas. Between 1990 and 1993, the number of overstayers, according to official figures, increased from 106,000 to 297,000.[26] Three-quarters of the overstayers come from six countries: Thailand, The Republic of Korea, Malaysia, Philippines, the Islamic Republic of Iran, and China.

Rapid economic growth elsewhere in East and Southeast Asia has also stimulated many new migration flows. The newly industrializing economies (NIEs) of Singapore, Hong Kong (China), the Republic of Korea, and Taiwan (China) have all attracted immigrant workers. Like Japan, they have been determined to increase levels of technology to avoid labor shortages, but have nevertheless had to permit immigration, particularly for industries such as construction that demand large numbers of unskilled workers. All have tried to control the inflow. Singapore has the tightest system. The country in 1995 had about 350,000 foreign workers—making up 21 percent of the labor force—and imposed severe sanctions on employers of undocumented immigrants. But even here there are reports of increasing numbers of undocumented workers.[27]

Following in their footsteps are the next generation of NIEs, notably Thailand and Malaysia. Here, however, the flows are even more complex—these countries are both sources and destinations for migrant workers. Thailand is host to 600,000 migrants, but also has 372,000 Thai workers spread around Asia.[28] In 1996 there were 120,000 Thai workers in Taiwan (China), for example, many building expressways in Taipei, while in northern Thailand there were thousands of Burmese workers helping to build a stadium to host the Asian Games.[29] Given the complexity and extent of these flows, the number of migrants in East Asia in total has been estimated at 2.6 million.[30] Following the financial crisis in Asia, there were pressures for these migrants to return. Many did so, but as with countries that industrialized earlier, even the NIEs are discovering that the immigrant work force has become structurally embedded in their economies and societies and will not necessarily disappear even during a period of recession. This an issue that is discussed further in Chapter 10.

Other Flows

Labor migration is truly a global phenomenon and other regions are also seeing constantly shifting patterns of migration.

- *Africa* has traditionally seen people moving across national frontiers—indeed often ignoring them—to work in mines and plantations. One of the most consistent patterns is of people moving from the remoter inland regions and countries to those closer to the coast. Some of the highest concentrations are in West Africa, moving to the richer countries such as Côte d'Ivoire and Nigeria.[31] In Southern Africa, South Africa has always been a magnet, but flows of undocumented workers have increased markedly in the postapartheid era. As in most countries, the numbers of undocumented immigrants are a matter of some dispute. The Department of Home Affairs estimated in 1995 that the number of undocumented immigrants in the country was about 3 million, but other estimates go as high as 8 million (20 percent of the population)—most of whom come from Mozambique, Zimbabwe, and Lesotho.[32]
- *Former Soviet Union and Eastern Europe*—The political upheavals in this region also generated large flows of migrants. More than 9 million former Soviet citizens moved following the collapse of the Soviet system. Many of these were fleeing fighting,

or were Russians who had moved to what had become other republics and found themselves unwelcome—some 2.7 million of these are believed to have moved to Russia between 1993 and 1996.[33] But others have moved in search of work. In 1996 there were reportedly 350,000 legal foreign workers in Russia. Around 60,000 of these are in Moscow—of whom one-third are from Ukraine. However, in addition to these, Moscow was also thought to have 400,000 undocumented foreign workers.[34] In addition to migration within Eastern Europe, these countries have also become staging posts for migrants seeking an easier entry to Western Europe.

- *Latin America*—The dominant migration flows are northward to the United States. But there is also a slower flow to Argentina, Brazil, and Mexico from neighboring countries. Argentina, for example, has an estimated 200,000 undocumented immigrants from Peru, Bolivia, and Paraguay. Mexico draws in Central Americans, many of whom are heading further north, but higher wages in Mexico's southern states also attract immigrants from Guatemala to work on coffee plantations, or in construction, or in domestic service.

Refugees

International labor flows have always been mixed with those of refugees. This is not only because the same conflicts that produce political refugees also create economic disruption and poverty, but also because many people in recent years have claimed refugee status as a way of bypassing immigration controls. Following the breakup of the Soviet Union, and the war in former Yugoslavia, the annual number of asylum seekers, which in the 1970s had only been about 30,000, had by 1992 risen to 800,000.

A few asylum seekers succeed. But even those who fail often become immigrant workers. It may take months or years to process the claims of asylum seekers, and in the meantime many are allowed to work. It is, moreover, difficult to deport those who are refused asylum. In Europe in 1994, of a total of 481,000 applications adjudicated, only 10 percent were accepted, but a further 12 percent were ultimately allowed to remain for humanitarian reasons. As a result of these pressures, European countries have steadily been raising barriers to asylum, including imposing visa requirements and sanctions on airlines, as well as refusing to accept people who have transited through a third country judged to be "safe."[35] This tighter environment has deterred many potential applicants. As Figure 3.3 indicates, the number of applications to Europe, North America, and Australia has dropped sharply and by 1998 was down to 350,000.

Figure 3.3   Asylum Applications to IGC States, 1984–1998

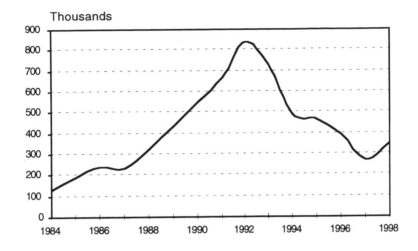

Thousands

Source: Inter-Governmental Consultations on Asylum, Refugee and Migration Policies in Europe, North America and Australia (IGC), 1999.

Conclusion

Current patterns of international migration are now very diverse. They respond to wide wage disparities between rich and poor countries, but these disparities are not static; in recent decades countries such as Pakistan and the Republic of Korea, which previously were economically equivalent, are moving ever further apart.

While migration flows are generated primarily by wage differences, they are also distorted by social and political pressures as host communities become more resistant to new arrivals. As a result, some of the traditional migration channels, particularly from Europe, have dried up, while many new ones are being created, notably in Southeast Asia. What effect will the current phase of globalization have on these new patterns? The next chapter examines the possibility that the increased flow of goods may eventually substitute for the flow of people.

Notes

1. United Press International. 1996.
2. *Migration News,* vol. 3, no. 8. (DM stands for Deutschmarks.)
3. Ibid., vol. 4, no. 12.
4. Morgan Stanley & Co., Inc. 1996, p. 12.
5. Massey, D., et al. 1993, p. 217.

6. *Migration News,* vol. 3, no. 11.

7. Avila, J. 1998, p. 1.

8. Hanson, G., and A. Spilimbergo. 1996, p. 1.

9. Massey, D. 1988.

10. Goss, J., and B. Lindquist. 1995, p. 321.

11. Freeman, R. 1993, p. 444.

12. Stahl, C. 1995, p. 211.

13. Werner, H. 1996, p. 166.

14. Cose, E. 1992, p. 105.

15. U.S. Immigration and Naturalization Service, 1997.

16. Economic Council of Canada. 1991, p. 4.

17. Bureau of Immigration Research. 1996. *Immigration Update, March Quarter,* Canberra, p. 23.

18. Hiro, D. 1992, p. 17.

19. Hollifield, J. 1992.

20. Stalker, P. 1994, p. 17.

21. Münz, R., and R. Ulrich. 1998.

22. Economic and Social Commission for Western Asia (ESCWA). 1993.

23. Jehl, D. 1996.

24. Mahmood, R. 1996, p. 98.

25. *Migration News,* vol. 3, no. 8.

26. SOPEMI/OECD. 1995, p. 100.

27. Wong, D. 1997, p. 140.

28. Silverman, G. 1996.

29. Janchitfah, S. 1995.

30. Silverman, G. 1996.

31. Adepojou, A, 1995, p. 93.

32. Reitzes, M. 1995, p. 2.

33. Bennett Jones, O. 1996.

34. *Migration News,* vol. 3, no. 9.

35. UNHCR. 1995.

4

Sending Goods
Instead of People

One of the most significant aspects of globalization has been a steady increase in international trade. Could this reduce the need for people to travel overseas in search of work? Could they not stay at home and send products instead? Instead of Bangladeshi textile workers traveling to Tokyo to work in Japanese factories, they could stay in Dhaka and send shirts to Japan.

The standard neoclassical trade theory (the Heckscher-Ohlin model) says that this is what ought to happen. Countries should produce and export those goods in which they have a comparative advantage. This advantage will be determined by how well endowed they are with capital, labor, natural resources, or technology. Bangladesh is well endowed with the cheap labor required for the relatively low-tech activity of stitching shirts. Japan, on the other hand, has plenty of the capital required to produce automobiles, which explains the large number of Toyotas on the streets of Dhaka. In the end, trade should substitute for migration.

The Real World

As with most predictions of neoclassical economics, the idea that trade should substitute for migration involves a number of assumptions distant from conditions in the real world. The most significant is that adjustment will take time. Even if governments are keen to make changes, they will come up against vested interests—employers and workers who may resist, or at least slow down, the removal of trade barriers. The textile and garment industries are the most striking examples. Even if employers are willing, it can be a slow process. Entrepreneurs in rich countries will need time to stop producing labor-intensive goods (sometimes with immigrant labor) and move to more capital-intensive production. Entrepreneurs in poor countries will need time to switch from capital-intensive goods that previously had been protected and move over to labor-intensive goods for which there is now a greater market overseas.

But in addition to the time lag, there are other reasons that the gains may not be as rapid or as great as hoped. Though developing countries have plenty of cheap labor, they have deficiencies that will reduce their productivity and their international competitiveness. Labor-rich countries typically suffer from poor infrastructure, such as roads and telecommunications, that hamper the speed with which they can respond to international markets. Additionally, their work force is poorly educated and trained, making them less flexible and less productive.

Even when the process of adjustment gets under way, it will not necessarily reduce migration. Indeed, initially it may increase it— first, because old industries are destroyed by international competition more quickly than new ones can be created, and because of this time lag between the loss of old jobs and the creation of new ones, people may be forced to emigrate. Then when new jobs are created, and wages increase, this will make workers more mobile and give them the funds to travel overseas. Only when development has been under way for some time will people have faith that staying at home is the better long-term option.

The result of these processes is what has been called a "migration hump" as emigration initially rises and later falls. This syndrome, which is covered in greater detail in Chapter 6, is not a consequence of trade alone, but trade will certainly play a part. The rest of this chapter is devoted to changes in trade patterns in the short and medium term, and their likely implications for migration.

The New, New Economic Order

In the long term, trade liberalization should enable greater employment in developing countries. Indeed, the prospect that this might happen is already creating considerable anxiety in the industrial countries. The European Commission in its 1994 White Paper, *Growth, Competitiveness and Employment,* giving a list of reasons that Europe still had 12 million people unemployed at a time when its economy was going strong, concluded: "Finally, and more especially, the countries of the south are stirring and competing with us—even in our own markets—at cost levels which we simply cannot match."[1] In the United States, the same concerns have been expressed with respect to the North American Free Trade Agreement. Presidential candidate Ross Perot famously warned of a "giant sucking sound" as jobs rushed south across the Rio Grande. Trade unions too have warned of major job losses—of around half a million in the first decade of the twenty-first century.

This is something of a turnaround from the fears being expressed a couple of decades ago. Then it was thought that the integration of world markets would widen gaps between rich and poor countries, leaving the poorer countries even further behind. Hence the calls for a "New International Economic Order" that would include greater flows of aid and commodity agreements to protect the poorer, raw material–exporting countries from the vagaries of the international markets. Many economists also argue that poor countries should raise trade barriers to protect their economies from exploitation by richer countries.

Since then the mood has swung dramatically in the opposite direction. This shift in opinion may be put down to a change in development fashion, or more charitably to the lessons of experience. However, it has been suggested that these fears may also correspond to different stages of global integration. Economists Krugman and Venables, for example, have illustrated how this might happen. They use a simple model with two regions, North and South.[2] Each produces two kinds of goods: "agricultural" goods, for which there are no substantial economies of scale, and "manufactured" goods, for which there are.

If initially the cost of transport between the two regions is very high, then both regions will essentially be self-sufficient and there will be very little trade. But as transport costs fall, the situation changes and trade will increase. If, for whatever reason, one region already has a larger manufacturing sector, it will be able to exploit this advantage. Not only will it enjoy economies of scale but it will also offer a larger market for the production of intermediate goods—making it a more attractive place to locate their production. As local production of intermediate goods increases, so better access to them will reduce manufacturing costs. Because of these linkages, this simple world will organize itself into an industrial core and a deindustrialized periphery. This differentiation of roles will cause labor markets to diverge. In the core area the demand for labor will increase, and in the periphery the demand will fall. Global integration will thus produce uneven development.

But if transport costs fall still further, then the situation will change again—in two ways. First, having intermediate goods produced close to manufactured goods becomes less of an advantage. Second, the peripheral region, with the advantage of lower wage rates, will look attractive to producers. As transport costs fall, the disadvantage of distance from markets will at some point be offset by lower wage rates in the periphery. Manufacturing can thus shift from the core to the periphery—and wage rates between the two will start to converge.

This simplified model differs of course from the real world in quite a few ways. There was never a time when all countries were equal: most developing countries have always trailed behind industrial countries. Even when their industry was undermined by the richer nations, this was often achieved more by colonial fiat than by market forces—as happened when Britain destroyed India's textile industry. Nevertheless, it is a plausible description of how nascent industrial development in poorer countries might have been stifled. Thus both historical and contemporary fears could be justified—the earlier fears that developing countries would be the victims of capital-intensive production and the current fears on the part of industrial countries of being undermined by cheap labor.

The Effect of Trade on
Overall Employment in Industrial Countries

Will trade in fact cause a massive shift of jobs from industrial to developing countries? At present, this does not seem to be happening to any great extent. Industrial countries may be facing increasing global competition, but it is not all coming from developing countries. Figure 4.1 shows how trade has risen globally. Exports from

Figure 4.1   World Trade, 1984–1998 (current U.S.$ billions)

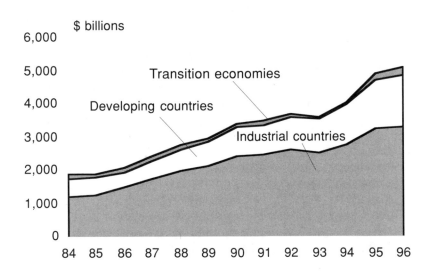

Sources: United Nations, 1994; World Trade Organization, 1999.

developing countries have increased, but this has not given them a significantly greater share. In 1984 they had 28 percent of world exports, but by 1996 their share had reached only 30 percent and fell in 1998 to 28 percent.

However, for developing country exports this disguises a fundamental shift in composition. As late as 1980, only 15 percent of developing country exports were manufactures, but by 1989 this proportion had risen to 53 percent.[3] The old pattern of trade in which the south largely exported primary products to the north—and imported manufactured goods—has been replaced by one where the north and the south each specialize in different kinds of manufactured goods. At the same time, as indicated in Figure 4.2, developing countries have been trading much more between themselves. In 1980, 67 percent of developing country exports went to the industrial countries, but by 1996 this proportion had fallen to 55 percent.

The effect of this in industrial countries is a matter of some debate. The rise in imports from developing countries, initially at least, has been concentrated in labor-intensive production that will have displaced low-skilled and unskilled workers in industrial countries. The most dramatic estimate suggests that the rise in imports from developing countries between 1960 and 1990 reduced the demand for unskilled labor in industrial countries by between 12 and 28 percent, with around 70 percent of this change occurring in the 1980s.[4] Other analysts are more conservative. They point out that in the early 1990s imports of manufactures from developing countries were

Figure 4.2   Destination of Developing Country Exports, 1980 and 1996

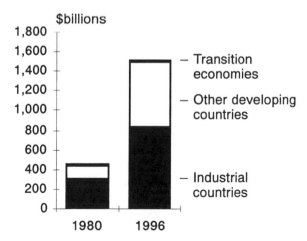

Source: United Nations, 1997.

only around 2 percent of the industrial countries' GDP and that the impact must have been more limited.[5] More recently, it has been suggested that the important issue is the elasticity of demand for unskilled labor. The argument is that trade has increased this elasticity, so although it may not have reduced employment it will have undermined the bargaining power of workers in industrial countries and made it difficult for them to demand higher wages.[6]

One reason that the effect on overall employment is small is that in industrial countries many more people now work in the service sector. The production of tradable goods—agricultural and industrial products—involves a declining proportion of the work force. In the Organization for Economic Cooperation and Development (OECD) countries as a whole, agriculture or industry now account for only one job in three, and the proportion has been falling almost everywhere: between 1960 and 1990, it fell in France, for example, from 59 to 35 percent; in Germany from 62 to 43 percent; and in the United States from 39 to 28 percent.[7] Thus, economies may have become more open, but those people directly exposed to foreign competition represent a steadily smaller proportion of the work force. In the United States, as a proportion of GDP, combined exports and imports rose from around 10 percent in the 1950s to over 20 percent by the late 1980s. But the proportion of people working in such industries fell.

Though the number of workers potentially affected is being reduced, many people—particularly the less skilled—are facing increased competition from lower-wage countries. Even so, the outcome will depend on the structure of the labor market. In the United States, where labor markets are more flexible, the effect is seen in a fall in wages, while in Europe the end result is more likely to be unemployment.

The plight of unskilled workers has certainly worsened in the OECD countries in recent decades. In all countries, unemployment rates for blue-collar workers have typically remained around twice as high as those for white-collar workers, with the ratio rising further during recessionary periods.[8] But it is difficult to say how much of this was due to imports and how much to technological change. In the United States, the rise in wage inequality between the skilled and the unskilled and the increasing ratio of skilled to unskilled employment have taken place across all sectors, not just in manufacturing, and not just in those industries affected by imports. This suggests that there must be another common factor, and a number of studies conclude that the most significant cause is higher levels of technology.[9]

In Europe, some of the most vigorous debate about the loss of employment to lower-wage countries has been in France. In 1993, some 12 percent of the work force was unemployed, and reports presented to parliamentary committees placed the blame on *délocalisation*—French companies relocating overseas. One report said that as a result, three affected industries—textiles/clothing, electronics, and footwear—had reduced their employment by half during the previous decade. But a number of other investigators have pointed out that such developments were also connected with both technological change and economic recession, and concluded that, even though some French transnational corporations had been investing overseas, less than 5 percent of this corresponded to the closure of production units in France.[10]

Overall estimates for the OECD suggest that the employment effect of imports from developing to industrial countries has been relatively minor. Estimates of the employment displaced by trade range from 1 to 9 million work-years.[11] A 1996 study of the effects of NAFTA on employment in the United States concluded that the net effect was negligible, or even positive—estimating that increased imports had killed 28,168 jobs while increased exports had supported the creation of 31,158 jobs.[12]

The Effect of Trade on Immigrant Employment in Industrial Countries

Trade is thus a contributor, even if not the major one, to a fall in demand for unskilled workers in industrial countries. But this impact will be absorbed by the whole work force, of which immigrants make up only a small proportion.

The proportion of foreigners or immigrants in the population and the work force is indicated in Table 4.1 for a selection of OECD countries.[13] These figures are not entirely comparable across countries because the definition of who is a foreigner or an immigrant is not consistent. In European OECD countries and in Japan, it is based on current citizenship status. In Australia, Canada, and the United States, on the other hand, it is based on country of birth. This will tend to reduce the proportion of "foreigners" in France, for example, where naturalization has been easier, compared to Germany, where it has been more difficult. These figures will also exclude the undocumented work force. Nevertheless, in broad terms this table indicates the proportion of immigrant workers, which among the larger countries varied from 17.9 percent in Switzerland to 1.0 percent in Spain in 1996. For most countries this represents an increase since the early 1980s.

The question then resolves into what proportion of these immigrant work forces are employed in sectors that compete with imports. This too will vary considerably from country to country. Almost

Table 4.1   Foreign or Immigrant Population and Labor Force, 1996*

	Foreign Population		Foreign Labor Force	
	Thousands	% of Total	Thousands	% of Total
Australia	3,908	21.1	2,238	25.0
Austria	728	9.0	328	10.0
Belgium	912	9.0	196	6.5
Canada	4,971	17.4	2,681	18.5
Denmark	238	4.7	84	3.0
France	3,597	6.3	1,573	6.2
Germany	7,314	8.9	2,559	9.1
Ireland	118	3.2	53	3.5
Italy	1,095	2.0	332	1.7
Japan	1,415	1.1	88	0.1
Luxembourg	43	34.1	117	53.8
Netherlands	680	4.4	218	3.1
Norway	158	3.6	55	2.6
Portugal	173	1.7	87	1.8
Spain	539	1.3	162	1.0
Sweden	526	6.0	218	5.1
Switzerland	1,338	19.0	709	17.9
United Kingdom	1972	3.4	878	3.4
United States	24,600	7.9	11,564	9.4

Source: SOPEMI/OECD, 1998.
Note: *Or latest available year: for Australia, Canada, and the United States the figures are for the foreign-born; population data for France are for 1990; labor force data for Belgium, 1989; for Canada, 1991; for Denmark and Italy, 1995; for the United States, 1990.

everywhere, immigrants tend to be highly concentrated in certain sectors, but these sectors differ from one country to another. In the United States the sector in which the share of immigrants is highest is agriculture; in Belgium and the Netherlands it is the extraction and processing of minerals; in Denmark, Germany, Australia, and Canada, it is manufacturing; in France and Luxembourg it is construction and civil engineering; and in the United Kingdom it is services.[14]

The United States

The effects of imports on the employment of immigrants will therefore vary considerably from one place to another. In the United States a study for the National Bureau of Economic Research analyzed the participation of immigrants in the production of traded goods.[15] This found first that, while as a whole immigrants made up 6.5 percent of the 1980 work force, they were more likely to be found in traded goods (7.8 percent of the work force) than in nontraded (6.1 percent). The analysis further divided the traded-goods sectors according to their export or import intensity—measured by taking exports or imports as a proportion of total shipments (those in the top quintile of export intensity were considered "high-export" goods; those in the top quintile of import intensity were considered "high-import" goods). For high-export goods, immigrants made up 7.5 percent of the work force, while for high-import goods they made up 10.4 percent of the work force.

Immigrants are thus significantly more exposed to foreign competition than nationals. However, the analysis also showed that black and female members of the work force were also disproportionately exposed. This is most evident in Los Angeles in the nondurable manufacturing sector, such as garments, where despite the recession, employment increased between 1979 and 1991. These industries were overwhelmingly dependent on immigrant, and particularly Mexican, labor. Mexican immigrants are thus overrepresented in industries that are at greatest risk from import penetration.[16]

Europe

The evidence on the concentration of immigrants in the traded-goods sector is less comprehensive in Europe, but it seems to point in the same direction. Europe as a whole is more dependent on international trade than the United States. As a proportion of GDP, exports and imports in 1994 were 69 percent of GDP for the European Union but only 27 percent in the United States and 23 percent in Japan. So one might expect a higher proportion of the European population to be affected by imports.

Moreover, immigrants can be even more concentrated in specific sectors than in the United States. An analysis of the labor force in 1982 found, for example, that 38 percent of German workers were in manufacturing, but in the case of immigrants the proportion was 56 percent, and that these immigrants were much less likely to be employed in the dynamic export sectors.[17] In France too, evidence from across twenty-nine sectors shows that immigrants are more likely to be found in import-competing industries (the sector with the highest proportion of foreign workers, 13 percent, is textiles and clothing). Similar results, though less conclusive, hold for Spain.[18]

Agriculture

Many of the industries that have demanded protection from foreign competition are also those that employ large numbers of immigrants. During the 1960s, it was predicted that there would eventually be no migrant farm workers in the United States, either because technology would advance sufficiently to render manual labor obsolete, or because production would simply shift elsewhere. But the combination of protection and an influx of migrants kept many agricultural enterprises alive. By 1991, the U.S. Department of Labor estimated that 73 percent of all workers employed in U.S. crop production were foreign-born.[19] A high proportion of these work illegally. Half of California's 700,000 farm workers are estimated to be undocumented. The need for such workers is at least tacitly accepted by the Immigration and Naturalization Service (INS). According to the California Institute of Rural Studies, between 1989 and 1991, INS agents visited just 32 of the state's 32,000 farms.[20]

Tomatoes, for example, are protected to some extent from competition from Mexico and elsewhere by a tariff of 4.6 cents per kilogram, as well as by nontariff barriers such as prohibitions on the sale of small tomatoes. Yet tomatoes in Florida are primarily picked by Mexican labor.[21] Avocados are another example. One of the major states of origin for Mexican migrants headed to the United States is Michoacan, where 100,000 workers are employed on 8,000 avocado farms.[22] Yet for many years the United States resisted importation of avocados from Mexico. Little wonder that former Mexican president Salinas pleaded that his country be allowed to export goods rather than workers.

The steady lowering of tariff barriers as a result of NAFTA should eventually shift more production of fruit and vegetables across the border to Mexico, but it is unlikely ever to displace migrant workers completely, and not for a long time. This is partly because Mexican production to a certain extent complements that in the United States—enabling table grapes, for example, to be available all year round. Indeed, Mexico's major comparative advantage is that it can produce fruits and vegetables during the winter months when production in the United States (except Florida) has ceased. The U.S. General Accounting Office has estimated that one-third (by value) of Mexican horticultural exports do not compete directly with U.S. production, and another 12 percent consists of products that complement U.S. production seasonally.[23] About three-quarters of U.S. labor-intensive fruit and vegetable output occurs when Mexican farms are not producing—so U.S. farms will always have an advantage.[24]

Nevertheless some production is already migrating across the border. One of the most affected crops seems to be broccoli—even though, through NAFTA, tariffs are to be removed only over a ten-year period. Fifteen years ago, Watsonville, California, was dubbed "the frozen vegetable capital of the world," employing more than 5,000 people in packing houses. Today the frozen-vegetable business has almost disappeared. This is partly due to a shift in consumer taste, but it is also because of a large increase in frozen broccoli and cauliflower imports from Mexico. Between 1980 and 1995, as a proportion of the U.S. broccoli market, imports of frozen produce grew from 3 to 60 percent.[25]

Thus there is some opportunity for agricultural trade to substitute for migration. Even so, the number of jobs likely to move may not be that significant, and some commentators suggest that it may take five to ten years for U.S. and Mexican investors to create significant numbers of new jobs in Mexico.

Textiles and Garments

In the manufacturing sector, the industries classically vulnerable to cheap imports are textiles and garments. These tend to be the first manufactured products that an industrializing economy produces. This pattern was established with textiles at the outset of the Industrial Revolution in eighteenth-century Britain, and in the nineteenth century in the United States, Germany, France, and the Netherlands. A similar pattern emerged later in these countries in the development of the garment industry. In the 1950s, the modern NIEs also started out relying heavily on textiles and garments—and they are now being followed by other countries in the Association of Southeast Asian Nations (ASEAN), as well as those in South Asia and Latin America. As a result, textiles and garments are the most geographically dispersed of all industries—across both industrial and developing countries.[26]

They are also very robust industries with good prospects—people will always want clothes, and the more money they have, the more clothes they buy. This has led to a dramatic increase in world trade. Between 1970 and 1994, global trade in textiles and clothing rose from $18 billion to $276 billion. Over the same period, developing countries' share in this rapidly expanding trade rose from 21 to 54 percent. Developing countries have made particular inroads in the more labor-intensive garment trade, where they are responsible for 62 percent of exports.[27] However, the distribution across countries has changed substantially over the years. As indicated in Figure 4.3, the trade is rapidly being taken over by China and other Asian economies.

Those enterprises that survive in industrial countries pay extremely low wages. About 70 percent of American garment workers are women, and their average hourly earnings in 1996 of $7.94 were well under the average manufacturing wage of $12.71. More than half of the 22,000 registered sewing shops in the United States were believed to be paying their workers below the $4.25 minimum.[28] Many of the garment sweatshops employ immigrants, and often undocumented ones. One of the most striking cases came to light in

Figure 4.3 Distribution of Developing Country Garment Exports, 1980–1994

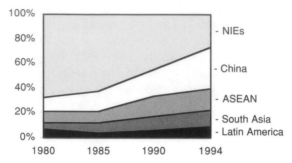

Source: Yang, Y., and C. Zhong, 1996.

Note: NIEs here are the Republic of Korea, Hong Kong (China), and Taiwan (China). ASEAN includes Indonesia, Malaysia, Thailand, Singapore, and the Philippines.

August 1995 when seventy-four Thai women were found imprisoned in an apartment block in Los Angeles, forced to work seventeen hours a day, seven days a week—and being paid $1.60 an hour.[29]

Faced with this kind of competition within their own borders, it is not surprising that garment manufacturers are choosing to locate production elsewhere. However, there may be limits to this. One reason for the persistence of sweatshops is thought to be that the higher fashion end of the industry depends on rapid changes in styles and needs to be close to the market.

Trends in the garment industry in Europe have followed a similar pattern, though some countries have done better than others. One of the most dramatic changes has been in Sweden, which has virtually eliminated protection from the clothing industry. As a result, over the last thirty years output has dropped by 90 percent.[30] At the other end of the scale, Italy is one of the largest producers, yet has so far been affected very little by imports. Indeed, at the beginning of the 1990s, it was the world's largest exporter of garments after Hong Kong (China). Italy's unique system of subcontractors seems to have helped sustain its industry. This was a remarkable achievement since its labor cost per hour has been the highest of the major industrial country producers—70 percent higher than in the United States. Employment that in 1980 stood at 169,000 fell by 1985 to around 140,000, then by 1990 fluctuated at around 150,000. Despite higher costs, the garment makers managed to maintain their competitive edge by improving quality and subcontracting to smaller producers—often to those employing undocumented workers. Most foreign investment by Italian producers was in other industrial countries to be closer to markets. When during the 1990s they came under cost pressure, they invested first in Eastern Europe and the Mediterranean countries.[31]

In later years even Hong Kong (China), the largest garment producer, was also coming under pressure and moving garment factory jobs to southwestern China. In 1995, unemployment among garment workers was almost 10 percent.[32] Taiwan (China) too has had difficulty recruiting and keeping garment workers at competitive wages—turnover in garment factories is 20 to 40 percent—and as a result many Taiwanese producers have moved to mainland China.[33]

In Latin America, production also relies on low-wage workers supplemented by immigrants. In Argentina, for example, there are an estimated 200,000 undocumented Bolivians, many of whom are working in Buenos Aires in Korean-owned textile factories that hire undocumented Bolivian and Paraguayan workers for as little as $300 a month for a sixty-hour week.[34]

The Impact of Free Trade on Emigration

What impact will the jobs "exported" from the North have on labor markets in the South? In particular, will they offer employment to those who otherwise might have emigrated? In the long run, trade might maximize employment. A simple calculation suggests what might be achieved. The sending country might, for example, be exporting goods in which labor accounts for 70 percent of value added, and importing goods where labor accounts for only 30 percent. If this country were exporting 20 percent of its GNP on these terms, then the balance of trade would be equivalent to the out-migration of 8 percent of its labor force.[35] This is clearly a substantial amount, but would not in itself be sufficient to stem migration completely.

Employment Losses Due to Free Trade

Free trade will cost developing countries some jobs in local industries that cannot compete. In 1990, 20 percent of industrial-country exports went to developing countries. By 1996 this proportion had reached 26 percent, and could have reached 30 percent by the turn of the century. In markets previously protected, and where there is no increase in local demand, this can lead to greater unemployment.

Manufacturing industry. Countries that have tried to build up local manufacturing capacity through protecting local industries will find themselves exposed to much stiffer competition. Mexico has already been through much of this process, even prior to NAFTA. After Mexico joined the General Agreement on Tariffs and Trade (GATT) in 1987, its average tariff on imports dropped from 45 to 9 percent, and between 1986 and 1991 merchandise imports increased by 20 percent per year. As a result, five hundred engineering firms in Mexico City alone went bankrupt.[36] While these job losses are serious, they are likely to involve fairly skilled workers who should readily find work elsewhere.

Agriculture. Rather more serious in its implications for emigration is the fate of agriculture. A number of developing countries are high-cost food producers, particularly of staples like maize that are grown on small family farms with little by way of irrigation or technical input. One country for which liberalization has ominous emigration implications is the Philippines. Following the Uruguay Round of GATT negotiations, the Philippines is replacing quotas on food imports by tariffs that will be steadily reduced. By the end of the 1990s, imports from the United States will be available at 30 percent below the current domestic price. By the year 2004, the gap will have widened to 39 percent. Oxfam says that withdrawal of import protection will put in jeopardy the livelihoods of half a million households—2.5 million people.

This is partly because U.S. producers are technically more efficient, but they do get a lot of help. Agriculture in the United States and Europe is heavily subsidized. For OECD countries as a whole in 1995, subsidies of various kinds were equivalent to around 40 percent of the value of their agricultural output. In 1995, the average per capita transfer to each U.S. farmer was $29,000—one hundred times the annual income of a corn farmer in the Philippines. It might be presumed that the Uruguay Round would have frowned on such subsidies, but not so. Agriculture remains one sector in which dumping is regarded as a legitimate trade practice. The implications for 1.2 million Filipino corn farmers are ominous.[37]

The Philippines government is less pessimistic about the outcome, arguing that the number of people who will lose out is much smaller, that competitive pressures will lead to major gains in efficiency, and that trade liberalization will increase average incomes. This is probably true, but the immediate effects on income distribution are likely to be negative because the corn producers tend to be the poorest farmers. The main corn-producing area is Mindanao, where one-third of all children under five suffer from malnutrition.[38] However, it may not be these families themselves who migrate internationally. Most people who leave rural areas in the Philippines go from poorer to richer regions where they start at the bottom of the employment ladder, while most international migration actually comes from the richer regions where people are higher up the ladder and have developed the necessary skills and contacts.[39]

Mexican farmers face a similar onslaught. Most Mexican agriculture is based on the production of corn and beans and operates very inefficiently. In 1991, 23 percent of economically active Mexicans worked in agriculture, yet they contributed only 7 percent of GDP—a proportion that has been falling steadily.[40] In the late 1970s, the government raised the prices guaranteed to producers (to about double the world price) and also raised the subsidies on imports, and then sold the products at low prices to urban consumers. After the debt crises, this policy was unsustainable, and since then there have been a series of reforms. In 1989, the government freed up restrictions on land ownership—reestablishing property rights, for example. But the reforms required under NAFTA are even more far-reaching. Mexico will have to dismantle its subsidies and move to international prices. This means that peasant farmers whose yields on rain-fed lands are only around one-eighth of those on the U.S. prairies will also have to struggle against the products of U.S. agricultural subsidies.

The prospects for small farmers growing maize are gloomy. Even when subsidized, Mexican peasant farmers were poverty stricken and for decades had been migrating to the cities and to the United States. But the removal of subsidies to around 2.4 million corn producers will drive hundreds of thousands more from the countryside. The higher estimates suggest that over 800,000 workers would leave the rural sector, of whom 600,000 would migrate to the United States.[41] By mid-1996, it was estimated that 500,000 to 750,000 subsistence farmers had already left agriculture.[42]

Not everyone in Mexico or the Philippines will lose out as a result of these changes. Apart from those who are geared up for export agriculture, local urban consumers are going to gain from lower prices for basic grains. In the longer term, there can be little justification for sustaining inefficient farmers. Nevertheless, the immediate effects on income distribution and poverty are disturbing.

Employment Gains Due to Free Trade

On the positive side of the ledger, migrant-sending countries will also gain from free trade in areas where cheap labor gives them an advantage.

Agriculture. In agriculture, for example, one of Mexico's opportunities as a result of NAFTA should be the export of more fruit and vegetables to the United States. This is an industry that is already well

established in northern Mexico. Even so, it may not expand sufficiently rapidly to employ many potential emigrants. One reason is
that capital requirements can be very high. This is certainly the case
for strawberries. California accounts for about one-quarter of the
world's commercial strawberries: annual sales now exceed half a billion dollars after a surge in production prompted in part by new
growing techniques, new plant varieties—and cheap immigrant
labor. Around half of total production costs consist of labor—strawberries are too soft for machine harvesting and need 2,000 work-
hours per acre, mostly immigrant labor paid about $200 per week.
The rapid expansion has been described as "not mechanization but
Mexicanization" of agriculture.[43]

Nevertheless, the strawberry business demands a lot of capital—
putting an acre of strawberries into production costs anywhere from
$12,000 to $30,000 an acre: a fifty-acre strawberry farm producing
high-quality berries requires an annual investment of at least $1 mil-
lion. At the same time, this is a risky business. Wholesale prices for
fresh strawberries fluctuate wildly, from $4.00 to $22.00 a box, depending on the quality of the fruit and on supply and demand. So,
although profits can be high (up to $20,000 an acre) there can also
be heavy losses, and growers who are to survive need deep pockets.[44]
Tariffs on fresh strawberries have been removed as a result of
NAFTA, but given that interest rates in Mexico are higher, and that
there are as yet fewer facilities for rapid shipment of perishable
goods, it will be some time before Mexico can take full advantage of
cheaper labor.

Even if this investment is made, the number of workers required
may not be that great. One estimate suggests that a 25 percent increase in Mexican acreage in fruit and vegetables in the 1990s would
involve at most 67,000 workers.[45] This can be compared with the
number of immigrant farm workers in the United States: a U.S.
Department of Labor Survey in the early 1990s concluded that there
were around 670,000 migrant farm workers in the United States, of
whom 85 percent were immigrants.[46] In 1990, total jobs in Mexico
based on trade with the United States were slightly more than 2.5 million out of a total Mexican labor force of 30 million (8.3 percent).[47]

However, the story could change. In recent years Mexico has, for
example, become a major force in tomato production—to the extent
that Florida growers in 1996 engaged in a "tomato war" to try to keep
out Mexican produce. In this case, Mexico's advantage was not
merely in cheap labor but also in technological advances that had
enabled it to produce a tastier tomato.

Labor-intensive industry. The garment industry again provides the clas-
sic upgrade path for the poorest countries. One country that has

benefited from export expansion in recent years is Bangladesh. Between 1982–1983 and 1992–1993, exports of ready-made garments rose from $7 million to $1.2 billion—going from 2 percent of total exports to 52 percent. The original impetus for this development was Korean investors exploiting Bangladesh's export concessions in European markets.[48] Garment making in 1997 was thought to employ around 1.3 million people, of whom 85 percent were female, mostly young and unmarried and earning around $400 per month.[49] However, the effect on emigration here is likely to be small. Though the industry is responsible for 50 percent of exports, it employs only 2 percent of the labor force. Moreover, this is not the group of people most prone to migrate. While some young Bangladeshi women do work overseas as maids, most emigrants are men. So the impact on emigration is likely to be indirect, and the direction is not clear. Either it will increase family income sufficiently that brothers will not need to leave the country—or it will give them the wherewithal to do so.

One problem for Bangladesh is that it has not been able to establish strong "backward linkages" between garments and the rest of the economy—there is not even much of a textile industry to feed garment makers with raw materials. There are a number of reasons for this, but years of political instability have not been conducive to building up the country's infrastructure, and the banking system is weak. This highlights a serious risk for Bangladesh and other poor countries. The garment industry arrived quickly and could well depart just as quickly—especially since as a result of the Uruguay Round it will lose its quota concessions and will have to compete with other, more efficient operators such as China.

The deflection of trade from one developing country to another is already being felt in the Caribbean as a result of NAFTA. While Mexico's exports of duty-free garments to the United States have been booming, the industry in the Caribbean has been shrinking. At the end of 1996, for example, a plant in Jamaica that had been sending T-shirts to the United States lost the contract to a Mexican company that could put in a lower bid. More than six hundred people (95 percent of them women) lost their jobs, and the Korean-owned company shipped the equipment to Bangladesh. A 1996 World Bank study suggests that the Caribbean could lose one-third of its U.S. exports as a result of NAFTA.[50]

Export-Led Growth to Keep Immigrants at Home

For countries such as Bangladesh, the most attractive trading path would be to follow the trail blazed by the NIEs in Southeast Asia.

After all, the Republic of Korea was until fairly recently a major ex-porter of labor. The exodus peaked in 1981, at which point there were over 150,000 Korean workers in the Middle East. However, as wages and employment expanded at home, labor exports declined steeply (Figure 4.4). By 1990 the total in the Middle East had dropped to only 8,000.[51]

This decline was the result of a rising demand for labor at home. The Republic of Korea and Taiwan (China) had, since the 1950s, been diversifying away from crude agricultural and mineral exports and rapidly expanding exports of labor-intensive manufactures, es-pecially of clothing and textiles, and of wood and paper products. By the early 1980s, in both economies, labor-intensive production made up more than 60 percent of exports. But over time, as wages rose with economic growth, their comparative advantage in low-cost labor was steadily eroded. This is illustrated in Figure 4.5, which shows the evolution from primary commodities (including food) to basic man-ufactures such as wood and paper products, garments and footwear, then to steel and shipbuilding, electrical machinery and cars, and fi-nally to high-technology products such as chemicals, pharmaceuti-cals, computers, and communications equipment.[52] The other first-tier NIEs followed much the same upgrade path.

The second-tier of NIEs—Indonesia, Malaysia, and Thailand—have been moving in a similar direction. Indonesia, for example, be-tween 1967 and 1994 increased textiles, clothing, and footwear from 0.2 percent of exports to 24.7 percent. The evolution of Thai exports is shown in Figure 4.6. Thailand had been even more dependent on primary commodities (food was the largest item). But here there has been no transition through metals and shipbuilding, and instead a more rapid arrival at high-technology goods. Malaysia has a similar

Figure 4.4   Emigration from the Republic of Korea, 1981–1990

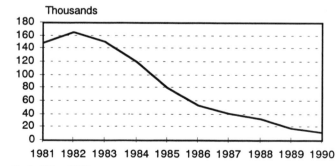

Source: Park, Y.-b., 1991.

Figure 4.5   Evolution of Exports from the Republic of Korea, 1965–1994

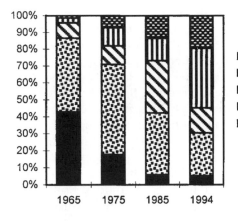

■ High technology
□ Cars and machinery
❑ Metals and shipbuilding
❏ Basic manufactures
■ Primary commodities

Source: UNCTAD, 1996a.

Figure 4.6   Evolution of Exports from Thailand, 1965–1994

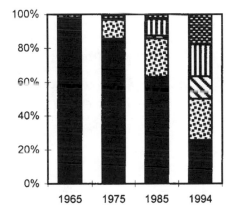

■ High technology
□ Cars and machinery
❑ Metals and shipbuilding
❏ Basic manufactures
■ Primary commodities

Source: UNCTAD, 1996a.

pattern, though with a higher proportion, 32 percent, of high-technology goods.

The second-tier NIEs thus seem to have followed a different path from the first tier. First, their exports are bunched more at the top and bottom of the skill ranges—partly because both Thailand and Malaysia are rich in land so that they can continue to export agricultural produce. Second, though these countries are engaged in high-technology production, their participation is narrower, since a higher proportion of the value of their exports is based on the import of previously manufactured parts. In the case of automatic data-processing equipment for the Republic of Korea, the import of parts represents only 24 percent of export value, while for Thailand the proportion is 79 percent.[53] To a certain extent, this reflects a new division of labor, with the second-tier NIEs assuming the more labor-intensive assembly states of high technology. As explored in Chapter 5, this is partly because their industries have been based less on building up local enterprises and more on attracting affiliates of foreign multinationals.

While the Thai economy had been booming until the Asian financial crisis, this was still not sufficient to cut emigration by any significant amount. As Figure 4.7 indicates, the numbers leaving were still substantial—similar to those for the Republic of Korea in earlier years.[54] These are official figures and probably a considerable underestimate. Many people are sent illegally by unregistered employment agencies, or leave the country as tourists and stay away to work. But as well as being a major exporter of labor (chiefly to Saudi Arabia, Brunei, and Singapore), Thailand is also an importer of unskilled labor (from Myanmar). The official figures for arrivals (175,300 in 1991) are very similar to those of departures, though again there are probably at least as many people working illegally. In terms of net migration, however, Thailand is probably in balance.[55]

The second tier of NIEs may, if they emerge from their financial problems, be able to shadow some of the experience of the original "tigers" in using export-led growth to stem migration. But this could take some time, and for the present they are in a very fluid position—

Figure 4.7   Emigration from Thailand, 1976–1993

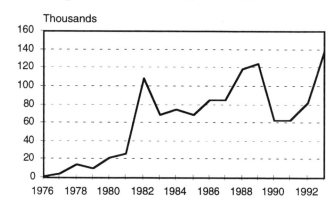

Source: Scalabrini Migration Center, 1996.

with many countries both exporting and importing workers. Like Thailand, Malaysia is also both a major importer and exporter, though generally it imports unskilled labor and exports skilled workers. Indonesia exports unskilled labor (to the Middle East, Malaysia, and Singapore) and imports skilled workers (mostly from India and the Philippines).

These and other countries that might want to follow the export-led growth path are faced with a world very different from the one that faced the original NIEs. In particular, the structure of industrial production has been changing in recent decades to reduce the demand for low-skilled labor in manufacturing. In many globally competitive industries, the share of low-skilled labor in total production costs has fallen from an average of 25 percent in the 1970s to between 5 and 10 percent in the mid-1990s.[56] In the case of semiconductors, for example, labor costs account for only 3 percent of total costs, in color televisions only 5 percent, and in the case of cars, 10–15 percent. The traditional labor-intensive options of clothing and footwear remain at around 30 percent, but competition in this sector is becoming increasingly fierce.[57] The reduced labor component can, however, be offset by an increase in trade volume.

New arrivals will also find themselves in a very different trading environment. With many more, and larger, countries trying to trade themselves into growth, there is a risk of flooding the market with excess production. This is certainly a danger for some products, but in the case of garments there is still some way to go. So far, developing countries have only around one-third of the market in North America, the European Union, and Japan—so if trade barriers fall, there should still be room for expansion without undermining prices.[58] Nor do they have to rely on industrial countries, since rapid growth in Asia is also a source of new markets.

What is less certain, however, is that the latecomers can maintain their competitiveness and eventually upgrade to higher levels of production. An analysis by UNCTAD looked at the proportion of developing-country exports that are based on sectors where imports to OECD countries are growing fast. For the first-tier NIEs, this was above 80 percent, but the second tier was still some way behind, with around 60 percent, and many other developing countries were making even less progress. Even Chile, which is regarded as something of an export success story, has only about 12 percent of its exports in such sectors. Indeed, of the developing countries in Latin America, only Mexico and Brazil seem to have an export structure comparable to that of the second-tier NIEs. As in the second-tier NIEs, this is based more on penetration by multinational enterprises than the expansion of purely domestic industry.[59]

Links Between Industrial-Country Exports
and Immigration

Countries that have close ties through migration also tend to be linked through trade—both connections are influenced by geographical proximity and historical association. The OECD has looked at the flows of goods and people in the 1980s between three groups of countries: France and the Maghrebian countries (Algeria, Morocco, and Tunisia); Germany and Turkey; and the United States and Mexico.[60] The data for France are shown in Figure 4.8. In all three countries, the share of imports from the migrant source countries grew over the period—though in France they started to trail off. However, there did not seem to be any correlation between the flow of goods and the flow of people.

There is also a considerable flow of trade in the other direction—with immigrants drawing in products from their own countries. Stores in the Mexican neighborhoods of New York and Los Angeles are packed with Mexican products—from mango juice to corn flour. The 32 million immigrants or people of Mexican descent in the United States represent a huge market. The Mexican company Grupo Modelo, for example, which targets its Modelo Especial beer at expatriate Mexicans, derived 35 percent of its 1995 income from exports to the United States.[61]

A further possibility is that immigrants may expand trade with their country of origin due to their superior knowledge of, or preferential access to, market opportunities. This proposition has been tested for

Figure 4.8   France, Immigration, and Import of Goods from the Maghreb, 1975–1990

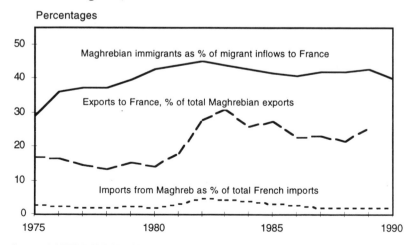

Source: SOPEMI/OECD, 1992.

Canada for the years 1980–1992. It was found that a 10 percent increase in immigrants from a particular country was associated with a 1 percent increase in Canadian exports to that country, and a 3 percent increase in imports. Among the primary categories of immigrants, the greatest influence on trade came from independents rather than via the entrepreneur immigration class.[62]

Conclusion

Given the currently fluid situation in international trade, it is difficult to project future trends with any great confidence. In the short term, free trade is likely to provoke even more emigration from poorer countries, while the longer-term effects will be more positive if trade helps the poorer countries restructure their economies to make better use of their labor force and embark on a more broadly based development path.

Also in the short term, free trade may stimulate further emigration because increasing exports from industrial countries will cause unemployment in some sectors in sending countries—particularly in agriculture. This is unlikely to be sufficiently offset by a reduction in demand for immigrant labor. Increased exports from sending countries could reduce some employment in labor-intensive manufacturing in industrial countries, and therefore the need for immigrant labor. But the latter effect is likely to be small because only a small proportion of immigrants—10 to 20 percent in most industrial countries—work in industries that will face more direct trade competition from poorer countries.[63]

The ideal situation would be a better balance between long- and short-term effects. If trade were freed up more slowly, this might reduce the disruption in poorer countries—and the migration—while still eventually achieving the long-term benefits.

Notes

1. European Commission. 1994, p. 11.
2. Krugman, P., and A. Venables. 1994, p. 5.
3. Wood, A. 1994, p. 2.
4. Ibid., p. 11.
5. World Bank. 1995, p. 56.
6. Rodrik, D. 1997, p. 26.
7. OECD. 1994, p. 4.
8. Ibid., p. 38.
9. ILO. 1995, p. 52.
10. UNCTAD. 1994, p. 188.
11. Ibid., p. 188.

12. Stevenson, R. 1996.
13. SOPEMI/OECD. 1997, p. 29.
14. SOPEMI/OECD. 1995, p. 40.
15. Abowd, J., and R. Freeman. 1991, p. 17.
16. Hinojosa Ojeda, R. 1994, p. 232.
17. Zimmerman, K. 1993, p. 31.
18. Faini, R., and A. Venturini. 1993, p. 438.
19. Cornelius, W., and P. Martin. 1993b, p. 9.
20. Sandoval, M. 1996.
21. Cornelius, W., and P. Martin. 1993b, p. 7.
22. *Migration News,* vol. 3, no. 8.
23. Cornelius, W., and P. Martin. 1993b, p. 7.
24. Martin, P. 1993, p. 103.
25. Tirschwell, P. 1996.
26. Dicken, P. 1992, p. 232.
27. Yang, Y., and C. Zhong. 1996, p. 3.
28. *Migration News,* vol. 3, no. 8.
29. *Economist.* 1995f.
30. UNCTAD. 1996a, p. 149.
31. Navaretti, G., and G. Perosino. 1992.
32. *Migration News,* vol. 2, no. 7.
33. Ibid., vol. 2, no. 5.
34. Ibid., vol. 3, no. 10.
35. Layard, R., et al. 1992, p. 55.
36. Stalker, P. 1994, p. 158.
37. Oxfam. 1996.
38. Watkins, K. 1997, p. 47.
39. Saith, A. 1997.
40. *Economist.* 1993a, p. 10.
41. Cornelius, W., and P. Martin. 1993b, p. 6.
42. *Migration News.* vol. 3, no. 10.
43. *Economist.* 1993b.
44. Schlosser, P. 1995.
45. Cornelius, W., and P. Martin. 1993a, p. 491.
46. Gabbard, S., R. Mines, and B. Boccalandro. 1994.
47. Hinojosa Ojeda, R. 1994, p. 230.
48. World Bank. 1994, p. 77.
49. Stalker, P. 1997.
50. Rohter, L. 1997.
51. Park, Y.-b. 1991.
52. UNCTAD. 1996a, p. 33.
53. Ibid., p. 120.
54. Scalabrini Migration Center. 1996.
55. Sussangkarn, C. 1996.
56. Oman, C. 1994, p. 17.
57. *Economist.* 1994.
58. UNCTAD. 1996a, p. 150.
59. Ibid., p. 125.
60. SOPEMI/OECD. 1994, p. 42.
61. Millman, J. 1996, p. 38.
62. Head, K. and J. Ries. 1998.
63. Martin, P., and J. Taylor. 1995, p. 9.

5

Capital to Workers, Not Workers to Capital

The previous chapter explored the possibility that the pressures for international migration could be reduced by an expansion of trade. Much the same question can be asked about flows of capital. Could flows of capital not only help expand production for trade but also stimulate local development that would increase employment and wages—and thus encourage workers to stay at home?

Most capital is usually generated locally. The fast-growing economies of East Asia were able to expand rapidly because they had high rates of national savings that could be channeled into productive investment. Other developing countries find this difficult to match, and lag way behind industrial countries when it comes to investment. In industrial countries, average capital per worker is $150,000, while in developing countries it is only $13,000.[1]

Countries that have embarked on strong growth based on local investment then become more attractive to outside investors. Mostly as a result of East Asia's dynamism during the 1990s, private flows to developing countries increased rapidly. Figure 5.1 illustrates recent trends showing how the character of capital flows has been transformed.[2] In earlier decades, more than half the capital arrived as official development assistance (ODA). The 1990s, however, have seen a steep rise in private capital flows, which by 1997 accounted for 85 percent of total flows—whether in the more volatile form of portfolio investment, or as private debt, or as longer-term foreign direct investment (FDI). This increasing globalization of capital flows could contribute to a dampening of migration—with capital migrating to workers rather than workers migrating to capital.

Equity and Debt

Since the early 1990s, many financial institutions and private investors have been attracted to the higher, if riskier, returns promised

Figure 5.1   Aggregate Net Flows to Developing Countries, 1990–1997

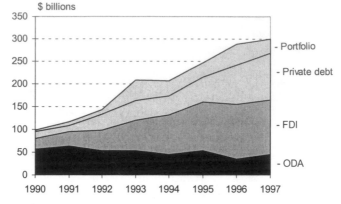

Source: World Bank, 1998a.

by "emerging markets." By 1997, portfolio investment in developing countries, which barely existed in the early 1980s, had reached $33 billion (down from a high of $46 billion in 1996) and commercial debt had reached $103 billion. While these may provide a welcome injection of capital, they carry a significant risk. If investors in equities lose confidence, they can sell their shares rapidly and the subsequent price collapse will reverberate through the entire economy. Further, if companies have borrowed funds denominated in foreign currencies, they remain sharply exposed to the dangers of devaluation. The inherent risks—and the implications for migration—were brought home first with the crisis in Mexico in 1995 and even more dramatically in 1997 with the onset of the Asian financial crisis.

The Mexican Peso Crisis

Mexico's economic boom in the 1990s was dependent largely on foreign savings. Domestic savings amounted to only 14 percent of GDP, and the current account deficit, which was 8 percent of GDP, was financed by foreign creditors.[3] Foreign investors held around 70 percent of peso-denominated bonds and 80 percent of dollar-denominated bonds.[4] In addition, in the four years to 1994 Mexico had attracted $64 billion in portfolio investment.[5] Unfortunately, not enough of these funds went into productive investment; instead Mexican consumers took advantage of the opportunity to stock up on imports.

As a result, the peso was considerably overvalued, and foreign investors started to speculate on when devaluation would come. Eventually the government had no choice but to float the currency and the peso lost about 50 percent of its value. The subsequent economic downturn hit Mexican workers hard—in terms of both lower wages and unemployment. Displaced workers started to make their travel plans—spurred by the knowledge that, as a result of the devaluation, the American-Mexican wage gap had risen from 8:1 to about 12:1. In January and February 1995, the number of aliens apprehended at the border rose 30 percent above the figure for the previous year.[6]

The United States was understandably nervous, not just about accelerated immigration but also about the prospect of losses in American jobs as Mexico cut back on imports. If, as predicted by one American bank, exports to Mexico were to fall by $10 billion, this could cost as many as 100,000 American jobs (it has been estimated that $50,000 in exports supports one American job).[7] As a result, the Clinton administration rushed through a loan package of $20 billion—of which the Mexicans eventually borrowed $12.5 billion. This seemed to do the trick. After a drop in output of over 6 percent in 1995, real GDP growth was above 6 percent by 1997. This recovery is evident in the continuing success of the *maquiladora* plants along the border. By the middle of 1996, there were 3,233 plants, employing in total 800,000 people—and they continued to open at a rate of two per day.

However, while the "dollar economy" was doing well, there are more doubts about the internal "peso economy" that continues to contract—and which is where most potential emigrants work. There must also be real doubts as to how effective the long-term cure will be for the dollar economy. Foreign borrowing soon started to climb again. By the end of 1997, private-sector external debt had reached 40 percent of exports—similar to the level before the crash—and by mid-1998 debt-rating agencies were warning that the sharp rise in borrowing exposed Mexico to "potential shifts in market confidence."[8]

The Asian Financial Crisis

Mexico's experience was to be echoed in a more unexpected part of the world as Asia's economic miracle came to an abrupt end. Following the sharp devaluation of the Thai baht in July 1997, the contagion rapidly spread to many other countries in the region with sharp devaluations and stock market collapses. Capital fled in huge quantities. Between them, Indonesia, the Republic of Korea, Thailand, Malaysia, and the Philippines in 1996 had net foreign-capital inflows of $96 billion, but in 1997 they experienced a net outflow of $12 billion—a hugely destabilizing switch that sent their economies into reverse. Growth in Thailand that was above 6 percent in 1996 was around zero for 1997 and predicted to be negative for 1998, and the other countries faced a sharp deceleration.[9]

The origins of the reversal are still debated—and there are certainly multiple contributing causes. In many respects the situation was very different than that in Mexico. Many of the countries had pursued economically sound policies in terms of fiscal balance, low inflation, high domestic savings, and open trade and investment regimes. The main weakness appears to have been poor regulation of a newly liberalized financial environment that permitted high and uncontrolled levels of foreign borrowing. This borrowing could have been avoided because domestic savings rates were already high at around 30 percent of GDP. Using foreign borrowing to push investment rates above 40 percent was both unnecessary and risky. Combined with overvalued exchange rates, this permitted cheap borrowing from abroad that often went into low-quality projects and property speculation. In Indonesia, for example, around one-quarter of commercial bank debt went into real estate.[10]

What is certain, however, is that the crisis was amplified by the speed of the reaction, and overreaction, of the financial markets—with collapses in currencies and equity prices that went beyond levels appropriate for correction—setting in chain reaction a series of events destined to increase unemployment and poverty. Unlike Mexico, however, many of these countries are both senders and receivers of migrants—often between each other—forming complex migration systems. The effects have varied between one country and another, but in the case of the receiving countries there does seem to have been an initial populist sentiment for expelling immigrants, followed by a later realization that even with high levels of unemployment it would be difficult to find local people to do the same work.

By the middle of 1997 there were thought to be over 6.5 million foreign workers in seven Asian countries and areas: Japan, the Republic of Korea, Malaysia, Singapore, Thailand, Hong Kong (China), and Taiwan (China). Estimates are shown in Table 5.1.[11] By mid-1998 the major labor-importing countries hit by the crisis were Thailand, Malaysia, and the Republic of Korea, and the worst-hit labor exporter was Indonesia.

• *Thailand*—Prior to the crisis, Thailand was close to full employment. But during the second half of 1997 at least half a million workers are thought to have been laid off from industrial jobs (one-third of these in construction).[12] The government was predicting that by the end of 1998 unemployment would have reached around 6 percent and, as a means of alleviating the problem, announced its intention to remove most of the million or more foreign workers (the majority from Myanmar). Around one-third of these had left by the middle of that year. However, some employers were protesting by

Table 5.1   Foreign Workers in Asian Labor-importing Countries

Importing country	Total foreign workers (thousands)	Number of workers by country of origin (thousands, latest year available, estimates of undocumented workers in parentheses)				
		Indonesia	Philippines	Thailand	China	Other Asia
Malaysia	2,500	755+(1,000)	100+(400)	79+(33)	n.a.	305
Thailand	1,260	n.a.	5	n.a.	60	944[a]
Singapore	450	100	60	60	46	n.a.
Japan	1,354	n.a.	84+(43)	18+(39)	234+(38)	680[b]+(88)
Hong Kong (China)	n.a.	50	120	18	n.a.	39
Taiwan (China)	297	9	84	138	21	n.a.
Rep. Korea	210	15	23+(15)	9+(6)	28+(49)	56+(20)

Source: ILO, 1998.
Notes: a. Mostly from Myanmar (Burmese). b. There were some 680,000 registered Koreans in Japan.

mid-1998 that they could not recruit enough Thais. Thailand is the world's largest exporter of rice, but the majority of workers in the rice mills are foreigners and employers say Thais were not coming forward to replace those who had been required to leave.[13]

• *Malaysia*— The crisis in Malaysia has not been as deep as in Thailand but has caused the cancellation of a number of major projects—with serious implications for Indonesian construction workers. At the end of 1997, the government announced that many foreign workers would have to leave, but by mid-1998 said that it would allow those working in jobs "shunned by Malaysians" to stay, including those in gas stations, cemeteries, golf courses, and retirement homes, and announced that additional workers could be recruited for manufacturing and plantations.[14]

• *Republic of Korea*— Until the onset of the crisis, unemployment had stayed below 3 percent, but by early 1998 was close to 5 percent and concentrated among first-time job seekers. In the early months of 1998, the government announced that undocumented foreign workers would be allowed to leave without being fined, and 46,000 took up the offer.

• *Indonesia*—Even before the crisis, unemployment was around 5 percent, with perhaps another 40 percent underemployed. In 1998, open unemployment could have risen to 10 percent or more. This has already resulted in increasing clandestine migration to Malaysia and Singapore.

Other major Asian labor exporters have suffered somewhat less during the crisis. From the Philippines, only around one-third of workers are employed in the region, and from Bangladesh about 80 percent work in the Persian Gulf.

Foreign Direct Investment

Compared with the more transient flows of equity investment and bank loans, foreign direct investment (FDI) has been more stable. Enterprises investing for productive purposes tend to be less swayed by short-term market downturns and put more emphasis on long-term growth rates and the opportunities offered by the globalization of production. This stability makes FDI a much more attractive option for developing countries where, between 1990 and 1997, FDI increased from 0.6 to 2.5 percent of GDP.[15]

With respect to migration, the potential impact of foreign direct investment is best divided into long- and short-term effects. In the long term, the issue is the extent to which FDI contributes to economic growth and thus makes the country as a whole a more desirable place to live. In the short term, the issue is whether incoming investment is directly creating employment for potential emigrants.

The Long-Term Growth Impact of FDI

The longer-term growth effects in turn can be considered in terms of the FDI contribution to capital, to technological development, to human resource development, and to trade.[16]

Capital. The additional capital from transnational corporations (TNCs) certainly contributes to growth. But on the whole FDI tends to follow growth rather than lead it.[17] TNCs are becoming increasingly choosy about where they will invest, and are generally going to countries that have already opened up their economies to international trade—and that also possess the human and physical infrastructure to take advantage of investment. This is why the bulk of investment remains in industrial countries. In 1995, of the $2.6 trillion global inward stock of FDI, 73 percent went to industrial countries. But in search of higher returns, TNCs have been heading for more adventurous destinations in the developing world. Between 1984 and 1989, developing countries received on average only 19 percent of FDI flows, but by 1995 this had reached 38 percent. Figure 5.2 indicates where FDI flows have gone.

As this chart shows, most investment to the developing world has gone to Asia and Latin America. What it does not show, however, is the extent to which these flows have been concentrated in a small number

Figure 5.2   Inflows of Foreign Direct Investment, 1990–1995

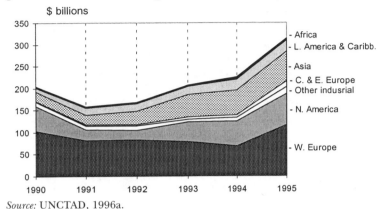

Source: UNCTAD, 1996a.

of countries. Of the flows into Latin America and the Caribbean in 1992, for example, 26 percent went to Mexico and 18 percent to Brazil. Of the flows into Asia, 55 percent went to China alone, followed some way behind by Malaysia with 9 percent and Singapore with 8 percent. Total flows into each of these last two countries were greater than into the whole of Africa.[18] TNCs tend to choose places with sound transport infrastructure and good local and international links, and the standards they demand are rising all the time.

The precise contribution to growth will depend very much on local circumstances. In countries that at present have little investment of any kind, FDI represents a very high proportion of fixed capital formation. In 1994, for example, this was 56 percent in Angola and 72 percent in Equatorial Guinea. However, even in countries where it is a very low proportion, it can make an important contribution in key areas of the economy. In the Republic of Korea, for example, in the period 1984–1989 inward investment averaged only 1.4 percent of fixed capital formation. But it was concentrated in key sectors: foreign affiliates accounted for one-quarter of all manufacturing exports—and in the electrical machinery and electronics sectors, their share was around 70 percent.[19] Moreover, the presence of TNCs stimulates the growth of local industries that are sufficiently developed to serve as suppliers.

Is this capital going to countries with the highest potential for outmigration? Historically this does not seem to have been the case. Most investment actually goes to net immigration countries. A number of significant migrant-sending countries, such as Bangladesh, Pakistan, and the Philippines, have not been very popular destinations for FDI.

Indeed, a much greater source of foreign exchange for these countries has been remittances from emigrants. One study calculated for a number of Asian migrant-sending countries how much capital would be required to produce the same contribution to GDP as migrant workers do through remittances. For 1989, this was estimated to be 1,020 times the actual FDI for that year in Bangladesh, and 25 times that in the Philippines.[20]

Nevertheless, there are other cases where FDI may be attracted to places by a combination of low labor costs, good transport infrastructure, and proximity to a richer country—characteristics that are also likely to provoke out-migration. This would apply to Mexico, for example, and other countries of Central America, to Eastern Europe, and probably in the future to the coastal provinces of China.

Technology. Beyond their contribution to capital, TNCs also bring with them the latest technologies. On the whole, TNCs do not transfer much of their research and development (R&D) functions to foreign affiliates. This is true even of investment in industrial countries. U.S. and Japanese transnationals investing in Europe are often criticized for transferring only such R&D as is required to adapt products and processes for domestic markets. Nevertheless, simply by introducing a new product or process, some technology and know-how are inevitably transferred. The technological convergence between Europe and North America in the 1960s that helped reduce the incentive for transatlantic migration was due in part to the establishment of foreign branch plants of American corporations.[21]

In the case of migrant-sending developing countries, the transfer of technology has been considerably less. In the mid-1990s, developing countries accounted for only 6 percent of global R&D (and without China only 4 percent).[22] In many cases, this has been because in the poorest countries transnational investment has been concentrated in export-processing zones isolated from the national economy. But even the "wired island" of Singapore only managed to spend a little over 1 percent of GDP on R&D in 1993—compared with 3 percent in Japan. Some of the Asian NIEs have been determined to step up their R&D, and the Chinese government wants TNCs to bring more technology with them. In 1996, for example, Motorola opened a $76 million computer chip plant and the Chinese government has been leaning on them to transfer more technology.[23]

The later developing economies are probably going to lose out in the technology stakes. A 1993 survey by the International Finance Corporation concluded that the pace of product and process technologies makes it less likely nowadays that more sophisticated production will be transferred to developing countries. As technology becomes more complex, so does the need to have sufficient high-level support skills available locally. This raises the prospect of an ever finer division of labor and a greater disparity between the faster- and slower-growing developing countries.[24]

Human resource development. In addition to providing capital and technology, TNCs contribute to economic growth by training their employees and by enabling the work force to make better use of their education and skills. Often they spend more on training than domestic companies—though this depends very much on local circumstances. When the Ford Motor Company established a new plant in northern Mexico, for example, all new workers received nearly seven hundred intensive classroom hours before starting work.[25] The training element will be particularly high for transnational service companies such as banking, financial services, and advertizing, which try to reproduce in host countries the same level of service as in their home countries. In this case, apart from using large numbers of expatriates, there is no alternative to training local staff. However, beyond formal training there is also a transfer of working culture.

Trade. Transnational companies improve the long-term trading capacity of host countries in many ways. Those that invest in order to exploit natural resources, for example, will add directly to the host country's exports. In 1992, American transnationals were responsible for 11 percent of raw-material exports from developing countries.[26] TNCs can also site production overseas to profit from the comparative advantages of specific locations. Originally this was based on exploiting cheaper labor, but with recent developments in technology and methods of production, many processes are being "sliced up" in a number of different ways. This contributes to a large flow of trade within TNCs. Currently this kind of intrafirm trade accounts for around one-quarter of total world exports. However, more recently there seems to be a shift to using subcontractors.

Transnationals also contribute to a host country's balance of trade by reducing imports. This kind of "market-seeking" investment aims to substitute for exports from the home country. By 1993, total sales by TNCs of products made outside their home country had reached $6 trillion—considerably more than total global exports ($4.7 trillion).

One of the clearest examples of market-seeking investment combined with widely dispersed subcontracting is the personal-computer industry. Although companies such as Dell or Compaq usually carry out the final assembly stages in, say, North America or Europe, the total supply chain would involve many time zones and countries according to local specializations. Thus microprocessors might come from the United States, memory devices from Japan and the Republic of Korea, disk drives from Singapore, and mother-boards and keyboards from Taiwan (China).[27]

The Short-Term Employment Effects of FDI

The most direct effect on migration should come from the employment of potential emigrants. But, as indicated in Table 5.2, the direct effect is likely to be small. In 1993, total employment by transnationals was 73 million—only 2–3 percent of the world's work force.[28] Nor do TNCs appear to be expanding employment very rapidly. While total FDI stock increased almost seven times between 1975 and 1993, total employment did not even double.

The relatively small contribution of TNCs to employment is partly because they have generally operated at higher levels of technology and productivity than smaller firms. The largest TNCs have increasingly sought labor-saving technologies, and have been outsourcing many requirements to subcontractors—particularly for activities that employ unskilled or semiskilled workers. The American footwear company Nike, for example, subcontracts all its production to independent contractors in different countries. The company itself only employs 9,000 people in such areas as design and sales, but indirectly it employs 75,000 people.[29] Indeed, an analysis of the three hundred largest TNCs concluded that they are probably directly employing fewer people than they were at the beginning of the 1980s.[30]

Nevertheless, TNCs have an effect on employment beyond those people who work for them directly. In addition to subcontractors, there are other forward and backward linkages within the domestic economy that generate many other jobs. These indirect effects will be greater in some industries than others—higher in automobiles, lower in textiles— but on average the ILO estimates that TNCs employ indirectly at least

Table 5.2 Employment by Transnational Corporations, 1975–1993

	1975	1985	1990	1993
Total employment (millions)	40	65	70	73
In parent company at home	n.a	43	44	44
In foreign affiliates	n.a	22	26	29
In industrial countries	n.a	15	17	17
In developing countries	n.a	7	9	12
Outward FDI stock ($ millions)	282	674	1,649	1,932

Source: UNCTAD, 1994, 1996b.

as many people as they employ directly.[31] Even so, this would amount only to around 5 percent of the global work force, a fairly modest contribution considering that they control over one-third of the world's productive assets.[32]

From the migration point of view, the major concern is their impact on employment in developing countries. Here, when considered as a proportion of the work force, it seems to be even less significant—though more encouraging when viewed as a proportion of total manufacturing industry. Thus in Mexico in 1988, affiliates of foreign firms employed 756,000 people—only 2 percent of the economically active population. But some 516,000 of these were working in a manufacturing industry—amounting to 21 percent of Mexico's paid employment in manufacturing. In Indonesia, the corresponding proportions were 1 percent and 24 percent. Indeed, TNCs account for more than 20 percent of manufacturing employment in a number of other developing countries and NIEs, including Argentina, Barbados, Botswana, Malaysia, Mauritius, the Philippines, Singapore, and Sri Lanka.[33]

Export-Processing Zones

At first sight, the most direct connection between FDI and potential emigration would appear to be through export-processing zones (EPZs)—which can employ just the kind of young and mobile workers who are prone to emigrate. In 1990, there were over 230 EPZs in seventy developing countries employing more than 4 million people—45 percent of total employment by TNCs in the developing world. Production in these designated duty-free areas continues to increase. Not all EPZs are the result of FDI. Many are set up with local capital. Indeed, since the largest numbers of EPZ employees are in China (more than 2 million) and are working under subcontracts to firms in Hong Kong (China), the change in the latter's status to a Special Administrative Region of China means that the majority are now owned by "local" capital.[34] (In addition, in China there are 14 to 40 million more workers in Chinese Special Economic Zones).[35]

Mexican Maquiladoras

After China, the next biggest concentration of EPZs is in Mexico in the *maquiladoras*—more than 3,000 duty-free assembly plants, mostly stretched along the border with the United States. These plants have a direct historical connection with Mexico-U.S. migration. Until

1964, the United States permitted seasonal Mexican agricultural laborers to work in the Southwest under the *bracero* program. When this program was discontinued, the Mexican government in 1965 set out to provide work for displaced workers by encouraging the establishment of *maquiladora* ("making up") plants along a 20-kilometer strip of the northern border. These take advantage of a provision in the U.S. tax code for products whose components originate in the United States but which are assembled abroad. The products can be reimported with import duty due only on the value added outside the country.

This proved remarkably attractive to investors. From 16 plants in 1966, there were more than 450 by 1970, and by 1996 there were over 3,000 employing more than 800,000 people. The first investors came from the United States, but by the early 1970s Asian businesses started to arrive and the Mexican government widened the permitted area of operation so that firms could also locate in the Mexican interior. This rapidly made the *maquiladora* industry the largest offshore production operation in the world. Originally, the plants concentrated on simple labor-intensive tasks for the manufacture of garments, toys, and dolls. But the product mix has shifted over the years—first into televisions and other electronic goods, and more recently into chemicals and other types of manufacturing. *Maquiladoras* are responsible for just under half of Mexico's manufacturing output. The chief attraction for investors over other locations is the labor cost, which undercuts Asian offshore operations by up to 50 percent.[36] Mexico's devaluation in 1995 reinforced their competitiveness—wages and benefits in mid-1995 were $1.85 per hour. The job losses caused by the devaluation also provoked a fresh flood of workers to the border areas, most of whom seemed to find jobs.

While the *maquiladoras* certainly provided fresh employment, they probably did little to employ the ex-*bracero* workers. These had mostly been men, while the *maquiladora* workers have primarily been women. However, the proportion of men has been rising over the years from 21 percent in 1975 to around 40 percent in 1996, and skill levels seem to be rising. Strictly speaking, one should also include those employed indirectly, but this is unlikely to involve many people because these plants import most of their inputs from the United States and have few linkages with the local economy. One estimate suggests that for every two hundred *maquiladora* jobs only three other manufacturing jobs were created, though there were thirty others in the service sector.[37] Employment can also be compared with the rest of Mexico's manufacturing industry, which has roughly the same output but employs 2.9 million people—around four times as many.[38]

Employment of Women

As in the *maquiladoras,* EPZs elsewhere have shown a preference for women aged sixteen to twenty-five. In the Philippines in 1995, of the 200,000 people employed in such zones, three-quarters were women—though the proportion of women tends to fall over the years, as the zones become more capital-intensive.[39] EPZ employers prefer women because they seem more prepared to adapt to the monotony of the production line, and are more malleable and trainable—and will work for low wages.[40] In 1990, for example, a business group in El Salvador placed an advertisement in *Bobbin,* the trade magazine of the U.S. spinning industry, singing the praises of "Rosa Martinez." "You can hire her for 57 cents an hour. Rosa is more than just colorful. She and her co-workers are known for their industriousness, reliability, and quick learning."[41] EPZs have played an important part in incorporating women into the labor force. Most of these young women come from rural areas, attracted by the prospect of a cash income, though they get paid the minimum wage or less, and work and live in very poor conditions.

Export Processing Zones and Migration

The link between EPZs and migration is complex. First there is the issue of internal migration. Certainly the zones do seem to employ a large proportion of people who have migrated to that part of the country—though they may not be recent arrivals. Migration is more likely if the zones are in relatively remote areas—as in Bataan island in the Philippines. However, these new workers do not stay long. Working conditions are often tough and hours are long. These conditions contribute to early burnout, and relatively few women stay beyond the age of twenty-five.[42] Labor turnover at EPZs is very high—8 percent per month in Mexico—and hiring and firing practices are harsh.

A frequent observation about EPZs is that because they largely employ women, and most emigrants are men, they will not have much impact on emigration. While this may be true in Latin America, it is not so in Asia, where in a number of countries the majority of migrants are women—generally working as domestic servants in the Middle East, Singapore, and Hong Kong (China). In the case of Sri Lanka, for example, about 69 percent of migrants are women, for Indonesia the proportion is 65 percent, and for Thailand, 55 percent.[43] For these women, work in EPZs, or other transnational enterprises, might offer an alternative to migration.

In the more traditional countries, women who lose their jobs in such factories find it difficult to return home. One report from a zone near the airport in Sri Lanka, for example, found that women's chances of marriage were damaged because women who went on their own to the city were deemed sexually promiscuous.[44] Those who find themselves out of work may thus consider looking overseas for employment. Having worked in Western-owned factories, they might reasonably consider that they could work overseas for higher wages.[45] Nevertheless, in the case of the Philippines and Sri Lanka, where the majority of emigrants are women, there does not seem to be any evidence that they previously worked in factories.

The fact that EPZs employ women can contribute to the emigration of men. With most factory work in EPZs going to women, men who find themselves competing unsuccessfully with women can be attracted to jobs overseas. In the 1970s in Malaysia and Thailand, for example, out-migration from rural areas was increasingly linked to women's employment in EPZs and the emigration of men to construction sites overseas.[46]

The potential for EPZs as stepping-stones to international migration is probably greatest in the Mexican *maquiladoras*. These certainly do attract thousands of internal migrants from other parts of Mexico. But evidence based on interviews with *maquiladora* workers suggests that they have little interest in emigration. One study in Nogales, for example, found that only 1 percent of workers who had migrated there had done so in order eventually to move to the United States.[47] International migrants generally come from further afield and bypass the border region entirely.

Conclusion

Just as with trade, the effects of capital flows on migration are likely to be very diverse. In the short to medium term, which might last ten years or more, investment may so accelerate social change that it provokes more people to leave—and gives them the means to do so. Even if investment does in the long term generate more employment, the jobs created directly are unlikely to have a major impact on emigration.

Probably more significant will be the contribution to overall economic growth. This suggests that aiming for quick job gains through EPZs could be a short-sighted strategy. Better perhaps to take the more difficult road of encouraging broadly based investment that is better linked to the wider economy.

Notes

1. World Bank. 1995, p. 61.
2. World Bank. 1998a.

3. Summers, L. 1995.
4. *Economist.* 1995a.
5. Ibid., 1995b.
6. *Migration News*, vol. 2, no. 4.
7. Ibid., vol. 2, no. 3.
8. *Economist.* 1998a.
9. ILO. 1998, p. 6.
10. UNDP. 1998.
11. ILO. 1998, p. 28.
12. Ibid., p. 18.
13. *Migration News*, vol 5, no. 7.
14. Ibid., vol. 5, no. 8.
15. World Bank. 1998b.
16. Sauvant, K., P. Mallampally, and P. Economou. 1993.
17. Bergsman, J., and Shen X. 1995, p. 7.
18. UNCTAD. 1996a, p. 227.
19. UNCTAD. 1996b, p. 122.
20. Abella, M. 1991, p. 11.
21. Dicken, P. 1992, p. 392.
22. UNCTAD. 1996b, p. 186.
23. *Economist.* 1996a.
24. Miller, R. 1993, p. 17.
25. UNCTAD. 1994, p. 223.
26. UNCTAD. 1996b, p. 84.
27. Ernst, D., and P. Guerrieri. 1998, p. 195.
28. UNCTAD. 1996b, p. 29.
29. UNCTAD. 1994, p. 193.
30. Parisotto, A. 1993, p. 46.
31. Ibid., p. 64.
32. UNRISD. 1995, p. 154.
33. UNCTAD. 1994, p. 186.
34. Parisotto, A. 1993, p. 58.
35. *Migration News*, vol. 3, no. 6.
36. Fuentes, N., et al. 1993, p. 166.
37. Ibid., p. 176.
38. *Migration News*, vol. 3, no. 10.
39. Ibid., vol. 2, no. 8.
40. Lim, L. 1993, p. 12.
41. Barnet, J., and J. Cavanagh. 1994, p. 325.
42. UNCTAD. 1994, p. 203.
43. *Migration News*, vol. 2, no. 8.
44. Barnet, J., and J. Cavanagh. 1994, p. 327.
45. Sassen, S. 1988.
46. Lim, L. 1993, p. 12.
47. Kopinak, K. 1996, p. 223.

6

Reducing International Wage Disparities Through Migration

The previous two chapters have explored the possibility that flows of goods and capital would narrow international disparities—and thus reduce the potential for international migration. A third possibility is that in a globalizing world the movement of people might also have a self-limiting effect. Drawing off surplus labor from the sending countries could reduce unemployment in poorer economies and perhaps cause wages to rise, and the arrival of new workers in the receiving countries could correspondingly cause wages there to fall. As indicated in Chapter 2, the early period of convergence between Europe and North America was to a large extent due to migration. Will future migration have a similar effect?

The Effect of Emigration on Sending Countries

Emigration from developing countries, if on a sufficient scale, could ultimately remove excess labor supply, reducing unemployment and increasing wages. One study for the Republic of Korea, for example, estimated that emigration in the period 1978–1991 reduced unemployment from 6.8 to 5.5 percent.[1] Unfortunately, there have been no systematic evaluations of whether this has happened more generally, though there have been estimates for individual countries.

The Philippines. The Philippines is a country with one of the highest proportions of its work force overseas—though the numbers are disputed. In 1995, the Philippines Department of Labor reported on estimates of 4.2 million workers overseas. This figure is supported in outline by a recent estimate that there are about 2.3 million Filipinos permanently overseas, together with at least 1.5 million contract workers and an unguessable number of undocumented workers.[2] In the late 1980s, it was thought that overseas contract workers represented 2 percent of the Philippines labor force. If those working abroad illegally are included, then the proportion might be as high as 4 percent.[3] In 1996, unemployment in the Philippines was around 8 percent, and some estimates suggest that if all immigrants were to return home, then unemployment might rise to around 12 percent.[4] In practice, however, this mass exodus seems to have had only a limited effect on unemployment. Even during the late 1970s and early 1980s, despite more than 400,000 people leaving each year, levels of unemployment continued to rise. Nor did wages increase.[5] However, there does not seem to have been any rigorous assessment of what might have happened in the absence of emigration.

Bangladesh. An estimate of the Bangladesh overseas work force suggested that in 1986 around a quarter of a million Bangladeshis were working overseas and that these represented 1 percent of the country's labor force. Bangladesh is a major supplier of contract labor to the Persian Gulf as well as to other Asian countries. Around half of these have been unskilled workers, but given the levels of unemployment and underemployment among unskilled workers during the 1980s, this probably had little impact on the labor market. Even skilled workers were in relatively abundant supply, and most of these were construction workers who tended to acquire their skills on the job and could be replaced over six months. An examination of wage rates for construction workers did not suggest any significant rises.[6] Since then, however, as Table 6.1 indicates, Bangladesh's exports of labor have been rising fairly steeply—from around 147,000 per year in 1991 to 231,000 in 1997.[7] Assuming, as did the earlier calculation, that each emigrant spends on average four years away, this would suggest that the number overseas at the end of 1993 was around 700,000.

These data refer only to those leaving officially on foreign contracts. There are also thousands of Bangladeshis working illegally. A number will be in India or Southeast Asia, but most of their destinations are further afield. Taking undocumented workers into account, other estimates suggest that in 1996 there were 2 million Bangladeshis working abroad.[8] The latest labor force survey for Bangladesh (1990–1991) said that the total economically active population was 51.1 million, which would put the overseas labor force at around 4 percent of the total.[9] It seems unlikely that this would have much of an impact on employment or wages. Official unemployment in 1990–1991 was only around 2 percent, but underemployment (working less than thirty-five hours per week) was 23.2 percent, so even 4 percent of people overseas will not make much of a contribution.

Table 6.1   Asian Overseas Contract Workers: Official Outflows, Selected Countries, 1990–1998

	Bangladesh	India	Indonesia	Pakistan	Philippines	Sri Lanka	Thailand
1990	n.a.	141,816	n.a.	n.a.	327,771	n.a.	n.a.
1991	147,131	192,003	n.a.	147,145	456,300	n.a.	n.a.
1992	188,124	416,784	n.a.	195,985	504,355	124,494	n.a.
1993	244,508	438,338	n.a.	157,387	492,936	129,076	114,062
1994	186,326	n.a.	n.a.	114,019	494,757	130,027	145,216
1995	187,543	n.a.	120,603	n.a.	412,120	n.a.	202,296
1996	211,714	n.a.	220,162	n.a.	401,873	162,572	185,436
1997	231,077	n.a.	375,317	n.a.	303,649	149,843	183,673
1998	n.a.	n.a.	n.a.	n.a.	460,748	n.a.	n.a.

Source: Scalabrini Migration Center, 1999.

Sri Lanka. In the late 1980s, the labor force was growing at around 140,000 per year while emigration was around 60,000 workers a year, so emigration may have helped ease the situation. However, the impact on unemployment is also likely to have been reduced by the fact that emigrants would not otherwise have chosen to work. A 1990 study concluded that two-thirds of Sri Lankan women working in the Middle East had not previously been part of the labor force. Unemployment in 1990 remained at 14 percent.[10]

Indonesia. During the period 1989–1994, average out-migration from Indonesia was around 130,000 per year, of whom 60 percent were women in domestic service. Indonesia is the only Islamic country in Asia that permits recruitment of women for domestic work overseas. Their services are much in demand, particularly in Saudi Arabia. Most of the other emigrants are also unskilled or low-skilled. A survey for the ILO concluded that even if these migrants had been unemployed or underemployed, their departure would have had a negligible impact on the labor market, estimating that in 1990 emigration was equivalent to only 4 percent of the total unemployed population and 0.35 percent of the underemployed population.[11]

Turkey. By 1993 there were 3.1 million Turkish citizens living abroad—around 5 percent of the country's resident population.[12] But in terms of the labor force, the proportion abroad was even higher—over 6 percent. Almost all were in the European Union, with two-thirds in Germany alone.[13] The precise impact of emigration is hard to judge because data on employment and unemployment are difficult to analyse precisely. But during the period of mass emigration, around 10 percent of the population was jobless, and a further 10–20 percent was underemployed. In 1973, at the height of labor emigration, 6 percent of the labor force was working overseas, and most analyses suggest that emigration will have relieved unemployment pressures.

However, as in the Philippines, it was not the unemployed who were emigrating. Most Turkish emigrants had jobs before they left, and around one-third of these were skilled workers such as bricklayers and carpenters, so their emigration should have opened vacancies for others. In terms of wages, the data are not very extensive, but there does not seem to be any evidence that wages rose. The minimum wage (for those covered by social security) did rise in the 1970s, but the sharpest increases actually occurred after recruitment for work abroad stopped in 1973. Wages in industries such as mining that would be less affected by emigration rose faster than those in construction.[14]

Mexico. By 1990 it was estimated that at least 5 percent of all people born in Mexico were living in the United States. In the 1990s, much of this emigration has been a response to the economic crisis in Mexico. But in the late 1970s, emigration had also been rising before the crisis and there was a steady increase in real wages.[15]

Egypt. Emigration from Egypt has at times had a significant impact on the labor market. After 1973, large numbers of farm workers and construction workers started to head for the booming economies in the Persian Gulf. One estimate suggests that by 1984 the farm labor force had been reduced by 12.5 percent, and by 1985 the construction labor force had been reduced by 21 percent. As a result, wages started to rise. Between 1976 and 1979, real wages in private construction were rising by 22 percent annually and in private agriculture by 31 percent annually.[16]

Loss of Skills and the Brain Drain

Emigration can not only siphon off excess workers, but it can also deprive sending countries of people they actually need. This would be detrimental to economic growth and could also increase unemployment among unskilled workers. It is difficult to estimate the damage that this causes. It can, for example, be measured according to the loss in investment in education. For the almost 90,000 highly skilled migrants who left developing countries for the United States in 1990, it has been calculated that this represents a net loss in tertiary education of nearly $7,400 each, or $642 million in total.[17]

Apart from the lost investment, what is the impact on production? This will depend on whether the migrants' services were in short supply in their home countries. Often this does not seem to have been the case. Universities in the Indian subcontinent have regularly produced an oversupply of graduates. In 1990, out of India's 3.8 million pool of scientific-technical talent, 1.2 million were registered as unemployed.[18] The Philippines is another prolific supplier of educated manpower that its own economy cannot absorb. Other countries, however, particularly those in the Caribbean and Africa, are losing people they could make good use of. It has been estimated that between 1960 and 1987 Africa lost 70,000 of its highly skilled people (30 percent of the stock), mostly to the European Union.[19]

As well as losing professionals, developing countries are losing skilled manual workers such as carpenters and bricklayers. The Persian Gulf countries have attracted vast numbers of these. In India in the mid-1980s, around 40 percent of migrants were skilled, and around half of these were in the construction sector; however, this exodus is not thought to have led to notable shortages.[20] Similarly in Bangladesh, these skilled workers can be replaced in six months or so by recruiting from the pool of unemployed unskilled labor and training people on the job. However, in other countries there do appear to have been problems. Pakistan, in the 1970s and 1980s, was sending more than 100,000 workers a year overseas, of whom around 45 percent were skilled.[21] This produced serious skill shortages and a steep rise in wages in the construction industry, and along with this there was a decline in productivity.[22] Even today, Pakistan has an estimated 2 million nationals working abroad—about 2 percent of the total labor force.[23]

It does seem, therefore, that in some countries emigration has an effect on unemployment and wages, but given the size of the labor markets this may not be noticeable.

Effect of Remittances on Sending Countries

Another way in which migration can increase incomes in the sending countries is through remittances. Apart from their benefits to migrants and their families, these could serve as a stimulus to economic development and thus inhibit further emigration.

The total value of global remittances is indicated in Table 6.2. These rose rapidly from less than $2 billion in 1970 to almost $70 billion by 1995. Estimating these flows is difficult and there is no universal agreement as to how it should be done. The figures here are derived by adding up three categories in the International Monetary

Table 6.2   Global Remittances, 1970–1995 (U.S.$ thousands)

	Bangladesh	India	Pakistan	Sri Lanka	Indonesia	Philippines	Thailand
1976	6.1	4.2	41.7	1.2	1.9	47.8	1.3
1977	15.7	22.9	140.5	12.5	2.9	70.4	3.9
1978	22.8	69.0	130.5	17.7	8.2	88.2	14.7
1979	24.5	171.8	125.5	25.9	10.4	137.3	10.6
1980	30.6	236.2	129.8	28.6	16.2	214.6	21.5
1981	55.8	276.0	168.4	57.4	17.9	266.2	26.7
1982	62.2	239.5	142.9	22.5	21.1	314.3	108.5
1983	59.2	225.0	128.2	18.1	29.3	434.3	68.5
1984	56.8	206.0	100.4	15.7	46.0	351.0	75.0
1985	77.7	163.0	88.5	12.4	54.3	372.8	69.7
1986	68.7	113.6	62.6	15.8	68.4	378.2	85.7
1987	74.0	125.4	69.6	12.4	61.1	449.3	85.5
1988	68.1	169.9	84.8	15.8	61.4	471.0	118.6
1989	101.7	126.8	95.8	24.7	84.1	458.6	125.3
1990	103.8	143.6	113.7	42.6	86.2	446.1	63.0
1991	147.1	117.5	142.8	65.0	149.8	615.0	63.8
1992	188.1	n.a.	191.5	55.6	172.2	686.4	82.0
1993	244.5	n.a.	154.5	48.7	n.a.	696.6	138.0
1994	186.9	n.a.	n.a.	n.a.	n.a.	719.6	n.a.

Source: Migration News, 1998.

Fund (IMF) balance-of-payments statistics—"worker remittances," "migrant transfers," and "compensation income." However, the interpretation of these categories can differ from one country to another, and commercial banks may not report the data consistently. Not all of these flows go to developing countries. The top five countries in total remittances in 1994 were France, Mexico, Portugal, Egypt, and the Philippines—accounting for around one-third of the total.

One major weakness of these figures is that they fail to capture transfers that take place through informal channels. This may happen because the banking system in the recipient country is weak or inefficient. Or it may be that emigrants want to avoid changing money at the official, often overvalued, rate. In some cases, migrants will avoid official channels simply by carrying a bag of cash, or they may import expensive consumer goods. But the commonest way is to use parallel foreign exchange markets—such as the *hundi* system in the Indian subcontinent, or the "money courier" industry in the Philippines. Microstudies in a number of countries have indicated that only around half of remittances may travel through official channels: in Pakistan (1987), 57 percent; in the Philippines (1992), 50 percent. Similar results have been obtained in the South Pacific where unrecorded remittances amounted to 57 percent for Tonga and Western Samoa.[24]

While for developing countries in general remittances might seem relatively insignificant, for a number of countries they are a major source of income and foreign exchange. Egypt in 1995 received $4.7 billion in remittances—almost equaling the $6 billion earned from Suez Canal receipts, oil exports, and tourism combined.[25] Albania in 1993 received from the 600,000 Albanians working abroad three times as much as it did from foreign investment.[26] The Philippines, according to the Central Bank, received $7 billion in remittances in 1996 (up 42 percent on 1995).[27] Jamaica has benefited from a steep increase in remittances in recent years: between 1991 and 1997 they rose from 4.1 to 9.8 percent of GDP.[28] In these circumstances, it is not surprising that governments are grateful. In the Philippines, former president Ramos once went to the airport to greet thousands of workers arriving for their Christmas holiday visits—hailing them as "modern day heroes."[29]

The income from remittances has been a boon to many poor countries as a source of foreign exchange. But what effect does it have on the economy as a whole, and on future migration? A criticism frequently leveled is that remittances are used primarily for consumption rather than for investment—and are thus unlikely to have a positive effect on their home communities. Studies in the Caribbean, for example, found that remittances were largely spent on food, clothes, and housing. In Lesotho remittances have been spent mostly on consumption items, consumer durables, livestock, and housing.[30] A review in the South Pacific found that remittances were used in seven main areas: first, to pay debts (many connected with the expense of migration); second, for the purchase of consumer goods, particularly food; third, the construction or improvement of housing; fourth, for savings or financial investment; fifth, for investment in businesses such as stores or transport; sixth, on community organizations (primarily churches); and seventh, for social purposes such as weddings.[31]

Given the immediate needs of migrants and their families, it is hardly surprising that so much is directed to immediate consumption. The low level of education of many migrants will also reduce their opportunities to make more productive use of their funds. But even better-educated migrants will often find a lack of viable investment opportunities.

In any case, it can be argued that many forms of consumption, particularly on housing, better food, education, and health care, are a good form of investment that will lead to higher productivity. But even when remittances are used for what might be considered pure consumption, they can also bring economic benefits. Much will depend on the structure of the economy. If remittances are used to increase imports, not much will be achieved. A study in Bangladesh, for example, estimated that remittances of $610 million produced a demand of $351 million for Bangladeshi goods and services and generated at least 577,000 jobs.[32]

An assessment has also been made of the effect of remittances on the Mexican economy.[33] This started from an estimate of 2 million "migradollars" brought into, or sent to, Mexico annually in the early 1990s. This was allocated between different occupational groups: landless rural workers, small farmers, unskilled urban workers, and skilled urban workers. In total, the $2 billion of remittances were thought to be responsible for $6.5 billion of production in agriculture, manufacturing (including petroleum), services, and commerce. Figure 6.1 shows how these remittances were split between three of these different remitting groups, and the estimated multiplier effects that the remittances from each group had on four sectors of the Mexican economy. Thus, the $554 million remitted by those who had been landless rural workers in Mexico increased output in the agricultural sector at home by $567 million. This was because remittances enabled families to invest directly in farm production, buying tools, fertilizers, and other items that they could not otherwise have afforded. In addition, their remittances increased rural consumption and boosted manufacturing and services (particularly transport). Commerce also gets a substantial boost from remittances: some stores open only during the winter months when migrants return, while others stock up in anticipation of a surge in demand.

The multiplier effects of remittances may thus be felt throughout the economy, and can make a significant contribution to economic development that in the long term might reduce emigration. But it is doubtful that an increase in local income serves immediately to reduce future migration. It is more likely that visible signs of success in new housing and consumer goods stimulate others to follow the same path. Moreover, the increase in wealth in the community also makes it easier for potential emigrants to get the loans they need to travel.

The Effect of Immigration on
Labor Markets in Receiving Countries

The corollary to raising incomes in the sending countries should be reducing the general level of wages in the receiving countries—or at least slowing any increase in wage growth such that incomes in sending and receiving countries eventually converge. However, there are two main reasons this might not happen. First, immigrants may not

Figure 6.1   Multiplier Effects of Migradollars on the Mexican Economy

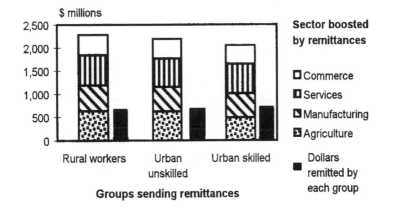

Source: Durand, J., E. Parrado, and D. Massey, 1996.

do the same jobs as the host population—but rather complement local labor. Second, immigrants are also consumers who themselves add to total demand—and being generally younger and more vigorous than the host society could serve as a stimulus for the whole economy. Thus, as well as taking some jobs they also create others.

Immigration During Periods of Fast Growth

The effects of immigration on the host country—and on the labor market—will depend on the state of the economy. Generally, fewer doubts are expressed about immigration during periods of vigorous economic growth. Germany from 1960 to 1973 is one of the most striking examples. Without the employment of young, motivated "guest workers" in the 1960s and 1970s, economic growth would not have been possible at the same pace—at least not without much higher rates of inflation, or moving production abroad. Initially, there was little objection from German workers. This was partly because of the general optimism inspired by a booming economy, but also because the Federation of German Trade Unions was closely involved in formulating policy on the import of labor. It managed to incorporate provisions that foreigners were to be paid wages equivalent to their German counterparts, and that hiring preference would always be given to German workers.[34] While less skilled German workers had their jobs protected, many others actually gained higher wages—a number of studies have shown that, as a result of immigration, many German workers have achieved higher professional positions.[35] Even for the years when active recruitment was halted, it has been argued that an increase in employment in Germany of about 3 million from 1983 to 1991 would not have been possible without immigration, and that the GDP would have risen far less.[36]

However, during the 1980s and 1990s, many other countries, also faced with booming economies, have adopted very different policies. Even with high rates of growth and severe labor shortages they have set themselves against the large-scale import of foreign labor. This has been partly for cultural reasons—they have pointed to some of the social consequences of immigration that have become evident in Europe. Certainly in Japan the objection to importing foreign labor has been as much cultural as economic.

However, countries like Singapore and the Republic of Korea argue that their best hope in a competitive global economy is to reach higher levels of technology and that the "easy" option of importing cheap foreign labor would delay this process. Singapore, for example, which has averaged 9 percent annual economic growth for the past thirty years, in 1981 announced it would continue to permit the entry of skilled workers but said that by 1991 it would have phased out all unskilled foreign workers except domestic servants and those working in shipbuilding and construction. This ambitious objective was abandoned in 1987 when it was realized that a carefully regulated pool of foreign workers could serve as a buffer against recession, provided they could, when not needed, be sent home. Singapore now has one of the most tightly controlled immigration systems—imposing stiff penalties on undocumented workers and their employers. To further reduce the incentive to use imported labor, the government imposes a monthly levy on employers—in 1996 this came to $312 per month for unskilled and $142 for skilled workers. Even so, immigrants in 1996 were still around 20 percent of the labor force.

The Republic of Korea has also attempted to take the high-technology road—but has been more resistant than Singapore to the import of foreign workers. Yet it still faces severe shortages that in 1994 were estimated as high as 4 percent of the labor force. This would translate into 250,000 vacancies—two or three times the stock of (mostly undocumented) immigrants. Some of the worst shortages are in the smaller firms. A survey in 1993 by the Korea Labor Institute and the ILO of 250 small and medium-sized enterprises found a vacancy rate there of 9 percent. Many firms complained of being unable to attract Korean workers, yet they were reluctant to raise wages for jobs at the bottom of the wage ladder since this would cause all wages to rise. Instead, many chose to employ legal or undocumented foreign workers at a little over half the wages of Korean workers. The government would prefer to increase national participation rates—in particular, to draw more older workers and women into the labor force. But around two-thirds of the firms in this survey said that older workers and housewives would be unable to undertake the intense physical labor. Even when employers had attempted to recruit them, the workers were unwilling to work for the wages offered. The other alternative is to replace workers through greater automation. However, most of the smaller firms shied away from this because of the cost and the risk.[37]

Other countries following in the path of the NIEs have adopted much the same objective. The Malaysian government's "Vision 2020" is that of becoming a developed country in 2020. This involves the promotion of key activities such as the microelectronic, automotive, aerospace, automated manufacturing, biotech, and information technology industries.[38] The employment of immigrant workers is seen as a necessary but temporary expedient. Malaysia in 1995 had an unemployment rate of less than 3 percent. Even so, the country was at that point still short of workers: a 1995 poll of 150 local, foreign, and joint-venture companies reported that 62 percent of foreign firms in Malaysia faced labor shortages.

As a result of these tensions, employers are often tempted to take on undocumented workers. Most Asian countries have significant numbers of undocumented workers, but it seems doubtful that they are exerting any significant downward pressure on the wages of other workers because in most cases, even when there is unemployment, they are taking jobs that local people refuse. Thus Taiwan (China) in 1996 had 200,000 undocumented foreign workers, mostly from China, while the unemployment rate was 2.7 percent—which means that 241,000 workers were unemployed.

Immigration During Periods of Slow Growth

Most immigration from poorer to richer countries nowadays, however, takes place during less buoyant circumstances, to countries that have much higher levels of unemployment and slower growth—and where there are understandable fears that immigrants are taking jobs from national workers, or at least are depressing wages. In principle, this need not happen, because migrants are themselves consumers whose employment will create demand for goods and services to be met by nationals.

One of the most straightforward empirical ways to judge the impact is to compare immigration flows and unemployment between different periods to see if greater immigration is associated with greater unemployment. An OECD study has carried out this exercise for a selection of countries, comparing the periods 1984–1989 and 1990–1995.[39] The results are summarized in Table 6.3. They suggest

Table 6.3   Gross Immigration Inflows and Unemployment

	1984–1989		1990–1995		Inflows increase (% of foreign population)	Percentage difference in unemploy- ment rates
	Average inflows (thousands)	Unemploy- ment rate (%)	Average gross inflows (thousands)	Unemploy- ment rate (%)		
United States	675	6.4	1,128	6.4	+3.2	0.0
Germany	520	7.6	920	8.1	+9.2	+0.5
Japan	183	2.6	284	2.5	+6.6	−0.1
Switzerland	69	0.7	101	2.9	+3.5	+2.2
France	45	10.0	93	10.7	+3.5	+2.2
United Kingdom	50	8.6	54	9.4	+0.3	+0.8
Norway	18	3.0	18	5.5	−0.8	+2.5
Luxembourg	7	1.6	10	2.0	+2.3	+0.4

Source: SOPEMI/OECD, 1997.
Notes: The increase in inflows is expressed as a percentage of the total foreign population (foreign-born in the case of the United States) in 1984 (1982 for France and 1980 for the United States). Data for Germany are for the Federal Republic of Germany until 1990 and Germany as a whole since 1991.

no direct correlation between the growth in entries of foreigners in a country and changes in the unemployment rate. In the countries with the highest increases in inflows, unemployment grew only slightly or declined.

This is a relatively simple assessment. However, there have been studies in individual countries that have looked more closely at the impact of immigration on both employment and wages.

The United States. In such a large country, one useful starting point is to consider internal migration between one region and another. The evidence indicates that interregional migrants create jobs: one study concluded that for two-thirds of the major metropolitan areas, each new in-migrant creates an average of 1.26 jobs—one for the migrant and 0.26 for others in the locality. It could be argued that the situation for international immigrants will be different since they may be low-skilled and bring little capital with them. On the other hand, international immigrants might bring greater benefits because they will also be increasing the consumption of goods produced by people elsewhere in the country, whereas for the interregional migrants net consumption would be unchanged.[40]

The United States is also the subject of most investigations of the employment impact of international migrants. Many studies in the 1980s concluded that immigrants did not reduce opportunities for national workers and in some cases may have improved them. These studies were based on comparing areas where migrants formed a substantial proportion of the population, such as New York or Los Angeles, with places like Nashville or Pittsburgh where they formed a relatively small proportion. Generally, the studies compared the wages and employment of three main groups—whites, Hispanics, and blacks. The conclusions were remarkably consistent: in most cases the effect was slight—even a doubling of the immigrant work force reduced the wages of nationals by only 2–3 percent.[41] The only groups that lost out were the previous cohorts of immigrants. A couple of studies concluded that a 10 percent increase in the number of immigrants reduced other immigrants' wages by 9 to 10 percent.[42]

Confirmation of this finding was obtained from studies that looked at individual labor markets before and after a large influx of immigrants. The most striking was the impact of the sudden arrival on April 20, 1980, of 125,000 Cubans who had been granted permission to leave Cuba. Overnight, this "Mariel" exodus (Mariel is the port from which they departed) increased the labor force in Miami by around 7 percent, yet neither the employment nor the wages of the labor force as a whole, even unskilled blacks, seemed to be affected.[43]

Most of the above studies have concentrated on individual labor markets. What they may not have taken into account is that national workers seeking employment may have deliberately avoided areas where they would find themselves in competition with large numbers of immigrants. California, for example, has been drawing in many immigrants as well as educated Americans from other states, but has been losing lower-income white workers.[44] In addition, more recent studies have concluded that, for other states of immigrant concentration, workers earning the lowest wages have been leaving. Looking at the economy of the United States as a whole, these studies have concluded that even if wages in aggregate were unaffected by immigration, workers at the bottom of the income ladder did seem to be losing out. One study concluded that there was a 10 percent decline in the wages of high-school dropouts, and that about one-third of this can be attributed to the immigration of unskilled workers.[45] Other studies have also suggested that low-wage workers have lost out—though not to the same extent.

On the other hand, immigration will have benefited many professional groups. This is partly because immigrants create a demand for all sorts of services, such as legal or administrative activities, that are dominated by national workers. But they also permit the retention of jobs that might otherwise have moved overseas: it has been estimated, for example, that without Mexican immigration to Los Angeles County between 1970 and 1980, about 90,000 jobs in industries such as textiles would have been lost.[46] Moreover, the availability of nannies and domestic servants releases many highly educated women to use their skills in the labor market.

Immigration could thus contribute to the increase in inequality that has been noted in the United States—though, as the President's Council of Economic Advisers reported in 1994, there were many other causes of the increase in inequality and it seems unlikely that immigration could explain more than a few percent of the total change.[47]

Canada. The evidence from other migrant-receiving countries seems to confirm that immigration did not have a severe impact on national wages. The potential impact of immigration on employment has long been a concern in Canada. Here the foreign-born make up 17 percent of the population, and in 1996 it was expected that there would be up to 210,000 immigrant arrivals, which as a proportion of the 30 million population is more than twice as high as in the United States. However, a number of studies emerged in the 1980s concluding that, when immigrants were considered together as a group, and looking at the labor market as a whole, they were not competing with the foreign-born—though when individual groups of immigrants were considered there was some competition (one of the most significant competing groups was immigrants from the United States). Another study, which considered workers by industry, also concluded that overall there was no competition, though in industries with a high concentration of foreign labor there was minor job displacement.[48] Other studies have also confirmed the lack of overall job displacement, particularly from Third World immigrants, but also pointed out that in some occupations Canadians face competition not just from Americans but also from Europeans.[49]

Australia. A historical review in Australia came to much the same conclusion. During the postwar period, regardless of economic conditions, immigrants seem to have created at least as much employment as they have taken. Looking at the recessions of 1974–1975, 1982–1983, and 1990–1992, a study from the Bureau of Immigration Research confirmed previous findings, showing that even during recessions there was no relationship between immigration and unemployment. Immigrants appeared to create as many jobs as they took; and the Australian-born benefited more from the jobs that were created.[50]

Europe. In Europe, there has been rather less research on the impact of immigration on wages and employment. One study from France concluded that all categories of immigrant are complementary to nationals and that a 10 percent increase in one migrant group or another would have very little effect on wages.[51] A study in Germany, similar to the comparisons between U.S. cities, also found little correlation between the wages of nationals and the proportion of immigrants in the work force.[52] Indeed, there are also examples where they have expanded opportunities for others. A study in 1991 produced by the *Land* (state) of Rheinland-Westfalen concluded that, between 1988 and 1991, immigrants had contributed substantially to the state's affluence by enabling German firms to make full use of their productive capacity. Far from crowding Germans out of the labor market, immigrants had created extra employment for them.[53] However, other studies in Germany come to a conclusion paralleling some of the more recent work in the United States, suggesting that there is a small but significant effect on the wages of those blue-collar workers for whom many immigrants are a direct substitute.[54]

For Europe, there have also been studies comparable to the Mariel flow from Cuba. The first was an analysis of the effect of the 1962 repatriation of the French from Algeria. But more recently there has been a study of the *retornados* to Portugal—the 600,000 people who in the mid-1970s returned from Angola, increasing the Portuguese labor force by 10 percent in just three years. A disproportionate number of the *retornados* went to urban areas of Lisbon, Porto, and Setubal. This study looked at the impact in two ways. One compared construction-industry wages between eighteen political districts. This indicated a strong effect—however, the timing and persistence of this difference suggested to the authors that there must have been some other factor at work. They were more convinced by their second analysis—an intercountry comparison with the experiences of France and Spain over the same period. This indicated that if there was an effect, it was a very modest one. Interestingly, this runs counter to the U.S. analysis that finds that there seems to be little impact on areas with high densities of immigrants, but a noticeable impact on wages at the bottom for the country as a whole.[55]

The effect of undocumented immigrants on employment has now become a significant issue in postapartheid South Africa. Previously, South African mines had relied heavily on labor from neighboring countries, but since then the proportion of foreigners in the mines has dropped: from 78 percent in 1973 to 47 percent by 1992. Recently, a more significant problem has been the arrival of undocumented workers, particularly from Mozambique. In a country where underemployment is 40 percent, this has fueled considerable resentment—particularly in the informal sector where immigrants are more likely to compete with local workers. The African Chamber of Hawkers and Independent Businessmen claims that there are 500,000 undocumented workers plying their trade in South Africa—representing up to 40 percent of the country's informal traders. Many others are taking jobs on farms where they are prepared to work for much less than local laborers. In some cases, they have been paid as little as R1.20 (about 30 cents) per day.[56]

The Effect of Immigration on Economic Growth

Even if the arrival of large numbers of immigrants does not appear to have an immediate effect on income for national workers, there is also the possibility that they will affect long-term growth. As suggested earlier, this will be positive if immigrants are meeting acute labor shortages. When they fill gaps at the top or bottom of the labor market, they enable local people to make best use of their own skills and thus increase productivity. However, it could also be argued that an alternative to immigration, particularly of the low-skilled, is to increase levels of technology and make production more capital-intensive. Immigration could inhibit this process, effectively "diluting" the capital-to-labor ratio, leading to a drop in productivity.

On the other hand, if immigration of low-paid workers leads to increased profits, this could finance greater capital investment. The latter seems to have happened in the Federal Republic of Germany between 1962 and 1972 when, despite high levels of immigration, there was an acceleration in the process of substituting capital for labor. In France, too, industries such as automobiles that hire large numbers of foreign workers also have a higher rate of capital-labor substitution than other sectors.[57]

Most historical research suggests, in fact, that immigration has improved total growth, even if the contribution is slight. A 1991 study by the Economic Council of Canada concluded that immigration enhances total economic efficiency within the host community—almost all of which derives from economies of scale. But the effects are small.[58] This link between economic efficiency and population size has also been emphasized in the United States. Studies in Europe, on the other hand, have suggested that even if total production goes up, this can be at the expense of productivity. But it is difficult to disentangle these effects from the structure of the labor market. If there is a shortage of labor for jobs that local people persistently refuse to take, then using immigrants to do this low-skilled work may reduce productivity, but without them the income of nationals could still have been reduced.

Conclusion

The question of whether international migration has an equilibrating effect that leads to a degree of convergence between sending and receiving countries thus remains fairly open. In the case of most sending countries, emigration is unlikely to be on such a scale as to create labor shortages that drive up wages. Nor is there any evidence that remittances are so stimulating development as to reduce the need to emigrate. In the receiving countries, this is a highly charged issue, but here too the evidence is inconclusive, and the effects if any are slight. In any case, it would seem that social and political objections to further immigration will arise long before it reaches such a scale that it has any major impact on the labor market.

Notes

1. Ghosh, B. 1996, p. 89.
2. Saith, A. 1997.
3. Pang, E. 1993, p. 57.
4. *Economist*. 1996b.
5. Goss, J., and B. Lindquist. 1995, p. 322.
6. Mahmud, W. 1989.
7. Scalabrini Migration Center, 1999.
8. *Migration News*, vol. 3, no. 12.
9. Bangladesh Bureau of Statistics. 1995.
10. Ghosh, B. 1996, p. 89.
11. Nayyar, D. 1997.
12. Fassmann, H., and R. Münz. 1994.
13. SOPEMI/OECD. 1995, p. 124.
14. Martin, P. 1991, p. 52.
15. Massey, D., et al. 1994, p. 710.
16. Abella, M. 1994, p. 173.
17. Griffin, K., and T. McKinley. 1994, p. 50.
18. McDonald, H. 1992, p. 46.
19. Adepojou, A. 1995, p. 99.
20. Nayyar, D. 1989.
21. Kazi, S. 1989.
22. Stahl, C., and A. Habib. 1991, p. 167.
23. Abella, M. 1995, p. 4.
24. Brown, R. 1995.
25. *Migration News*, vol. 2, no. 5.
26. Ibid., vol. 2, no. 1.
27. Agence-France-Presse. 1996.
28. Thomas-Hope, E. 1998.
29. *Far Eastern Economic Review*. 1994, p. 5.
30. Arnold, F. 1992, p. 210.
31. Connell, J., and R. Brown. 1995, p. 20.

32. Arnold, F. 1992, p. 210.
33. Durand, J., E. Parrado, and D. Massey. 1996, p. 423.
34. Hollifield, J. 1992, p. 60.
35. Mehrländer, U. 1994, p. 11.
36. Ibid., p. 12.
37. Abella, M., and Y.-b. Park. 1994.
38. *Migration News*, vol. 3, no. 9.
39. SOPEMI/OECD. 1997, p. 43.
40. Taylor, J. 1996, p. 50.
41. Tapinos, G. 1994, p. 157.
42. Fix, M., and J. Passel. 1994, p. 51.
43. Butcher, K., and D. Card. 1991.
44. Frey, W. H. 1994.
45. Borjas, G.. 1994, p. 1699.
46. Fix, M., and J. Passel. 1994, p. 53.
47. Ibid., p. 50.
48. Samuel, J. 1995, p. 11.
49. Roy, A. 1997, p. 159.
50. Castles, S., R. Iredale, and E. Vasta. 1994, p. 370.
51. Tapinos, G. 1994, p. 164.
52. Borjas, G. 1994, p. 1699.
53. Findlay, A. 1994, p. 186.
54. Zimmerman, K. 1994, p. 60.
55. Carrington, W., and P. de Lima. 1996, p. 330.
56. Minnaar, A., and M. Hough. 1996, p. 186.
57. Tapinos, G. 1994, p. 166.
58. Swan, N., et al. 1991, p. 36.

7

The Shock of the New

The fundamental cause of international migration is a gap in living standards between one country and another. But it takes more than this to make people actually move. They may, for example, be pushed by some sudden change in local circumstances, or they may be exposed to hitherto undreamed-of alternatives in other countries. Globalization contributes to both of these processes by shaking up settled communities, and offering new horizons that stretch way beyond the borders of the village or the nation.

The link between the disruptive effects of economic development and migration is well established. Mass emigration from Europe to North America and Australia from the mid-nineteenth century onwards can be fairly closely correlated with social and economic transformations—changes in agricultural productivity, a growth in rural population, and the onset in each country of the Industrial Revolution. People unable to find work in the countryside were driven to find work in the cities. Most of them succeeded, and remained in their own countries. But the process was very uneven, and many who found themselves shaken loose from the countryside, but unable to find work in the cities, had to try their luck overseas.

The correlation between emigration and the Industrial Revolution has been extensively researched. One study takes as a marker date for the Industrial Revolution in each country the year when railway tracks first exceeded 1,000 kilometers. On this basis, the wave of industrialization in Europe started in the 1830s in the British Isles; in the 1840s it reached France and Germany; in the 1850s, Russia-Poland, Austria-Hungary, and Italy; in the 1860s, Spain, Switzerland, and Sweden; and in the 1870s, the rest of southern Europe. On average, the peak year of emigration from these countries was twenty-eight years after this marker date.[1]

A similar process occurred in Japan. The period from 1891 to the 1920s corresponds to Japan's era of industrialization—and also to large-scale emigration to the United States and Australia. Even up to the early 1960s, Japan was the most important source of Asian immigration to the United States—a flow that abated only after 1965 with the onset of rapid economic growth.[2]

Pressures for emigration from developing countries can be linked to the same processes of uneven and disruptive development that are displacing people from the rural areas and drawing them to the cities. Here, though, as a result of technological spillover from industrial countries, the process seems to have been accelerated. Agricultural innovations, improvements in health, and the prospect of work in urban areas have provoked very rapid upheavals. The most obvious symptom is the explosive growth of cities—20 to 30 million of the world's poorest people migrate annually to towns and cities.[3] As a result, the proportion of the population of the developing world living in urban areas is growing dramatically: in 1960 it was 22 percent, by 1994 it had reached 37 percent, and by 2025 it is expected to reach 57 percent. By 1990, the world had some twenty cities with populations of more than 8 million, of which all but six were in developing countries. Mexico City is currently the largest, but others are not far behind.[4] This echoes the experience of the industrial countries around a hundred years previously. But the process in the developing world is altogether more rapid. London was the first industrial city to top 1 million, but it took 130 years to grow from there to 8 million. Mexico City has grown from 1 million to 15 million in just fifty years.[5]

Almost all these people are traveling, temporarily or permanently, in search of work. In most cases they do find it, or create it, if only in the informal sector at desperately low wages. In Dhaka, for example, 65 percent of all employment is in the informal sector, and in Bangladesh as a whole, half the population lives below the poverty line.[6] Migrants to cities generally trade one kind of poverty for another. Most will drift into squatter settlements where living conditions are miserable. Recent studies in ten major cities in low-income countries found the average family to have only 6.1 square meters of floor space, and 44 percent of households lack access to drinking water in their plot.[7] Once uprooted from rural communities, migration to another country is a logical next step.

This can also be traced historically. Mexican emigration to the United States, for example, has proceeded in a series of waves that correspond to different stages in Mexico's disruptive transition from an agrarian to a more industrial society. The first peak was in the 1920s after the devastation caused by the Mexican Revolution (1910–1919). Over the period 1841–1930, some 744,000 Mexicans emigrated to the United States—representing 4.5 percent of its 1930 population. By European standards, this was relatively modest; between 1864 and 1924, the British Isles, for example, sent 17 million people overseas—equivalent to 41 percent of its 1900 population. The second Mexican exodus began in 1942 and peaked in the 1950s, corresponding to a series of droughts and a lack of capital in rural areas. The third wave began in the 1960s, and continues today, closely connected with mechanization in rural areas that has reduced the demand for labor, and more recently with changes in land tenure. However, in each of these waves the number of emigrants has never exceeded 15 percent of the population. Given the pace of economic development, emigration from Mexico has, in historical terms, been surprisingly modest.[8]

Economic development has always been associated with emigration. To what extent has the modern phase of globalization changed the picture? Partly this is a question of scale and speed. Many of the processes that provoked emigration in the past have been accelerated. This can be seen from three different aspects: political, economic, and social.

Political Disruption

The political changes linked with globalization correspond to a weakening of national government control over many aspects of life. In general this has accompanied the spread of liberal democracy, which, though it permits greater popular participation, also raises the prospect of instability. Between two-thirds and three-quarters of the world's people now live under relatively pluralistic and democratic regimes.[9]

The most dramatic changes have been in the former communist countries—with the collapse of some states and the formation of many new ones. This in itself has increased international migration, particularly between states that formed part of the former Soviet Union. Between 1990 and 1996, more than 9 million people were on the move—one in thirty of the population. Many of these were fleeing fighting, but others feared discrimination—particularly Russians who had relocated to other republics and now found that they could not speak the new official national language. Between 1993 and 1996, some 2.7 million people returned to Russia.[10]

At one point, it was thought that the fraying of borders in Eastern Europe would also release a flood of migrants to the West. In practice this has not happened on anything like the threatened scale. There are a number of reasons: first, most people would not know where to go because there are no established networks for them to plug into; second, the cost of travel is more than many can afford; and third, Western European countries have tightened up their borders.

The most significant exodus has been of people who do have somewhere to go, and know they will be accepted—the *Aussiedler*, or ethnic Germans. From the end of the Cold War to the beginning of 1996, about 2 million ethnic Germans emigrated to their homeland. The scale of the flow was such that in 1993 the German government set a limit of 220,000 per year for ethnic Germans—and pumped huge sums into the former Soviet republics hoping to improve conditions sufficiently to encourage people to stay. In 1996, around 1.5 million ethnic Germans remained in what was the Soviet Union.[11]

Even if there has not been a mass exodus to the West, the loosening of state control on migration in Eastern Europe has resulted in a considerable circulation of workers between Eastern European states. Russia has become an area of net immigration. Moscow has a large immigrant labor force, with workers from Ukraine, Turkey, Georgia, Moldova, and Belarus. Many Eastern European countries are now both importers and exporters of labor. Hungarians go to work, often illegally, in Austria, while Ukrainian and Romanian migrants fill jobs in Hungary. The Hungarian Central Statistical Office reported in 1994 that some 120,000 Hungarians were living abroad, while 200,000 foreigners were living legally in Hungary—including 105,000 Romanians. Similarly in the Czech Republic, rapid economic growth is fueling demand for construction laborers. While Czechs head for Austria and Germany, foreign construction workers are streaming into the Czech Republic, mostly from Slovakia and the Ukraine. In June 1996, there were an estimated 100,000 Ukrainian workers employed in Prague.[12]

The more-porous borders in Eastern Europe, with chaotic controls and lax visa requirements, have also opened up the potential for using Eastern European countries as staging posts into Western Europe for immigrants from further afield. The Centre for Migration Policy Development in Vienna has estimated that 300,000 people are smuggled through Eastern Europe into Western Europe each year. Traffickers charge anywhere between $500 and $5,000 per person—earning an estimated $1.1 billion per year.[13]

At any one time there are a number of regular smuggling routes—though these change rapidly as standards of enforcement, and levels of bribes, rise and fall. For Central Asians, one established route has been through Russia to the Baltic states—often ending with a perilous voyage to the Nordic countries.[14] Africans and people from East Asia have been traveling via Turkey and Hungary. Poland is also used as a transit area—in 1995 the Polish government estimated that there were 100,000 foreigners waiting to smuggle themselves into

Germany. Gangs from Viet Nam and China also use Hungary and the Czech Republic as staging posts. This is made easier because thousands of East Asians came to Eastern Europe as guest workers during the communist era and have established restaurants that they use as fronts—police in Prague in 1995 raided a small Chinese restaurant that had 800 "registered employees."[15] Moscow is also a regular staging post, with Asians flying in on forged documents that cooperative officials choose not to inspect too closely. For those wanting to get to Italy, Albania is a favored transit point—they complete their journey across the Adriatic by speedboat—a route that has accommodated up to 50,000 travelers per year.[16]

Other parts of the world have also been going through political upheavals with implications for migration. In Africa, borders have always been very porous, with people passing from one country to another paying little heed to national frontiers. Here the changes linked with globalization have had more to do with the spread of democratic ideas that are creating even more fluid environments. In Africa in 1996, more than half the states were undertaking democratic reforms.[17] There are also links with the collapse of communism, since a number of African states were bolstered by outside aid from superpowers fighting the Cold War by proxy. These changes have undermined the centralized "developmentalist" state, allowing other divisions to emerge. At one extreme, this has forced millions of people to flee as refugees from war and genocide. But wars and emigration are also tied up with economic collapse—and people searching for work.

One of the most direct migration effects has been to accelerate the flood of people heading for South Africa. The apartheid regime had a fierce attitude toward undocumented immigrants—with a high-voltage electrified fence along its eastern border. The democratic government is now facing a fresh flow of immigrants. This is partly because the fences are not that difficult to negotiate. In one demonstration in 1995, an undocumented immigrant crossed in only one minute seventeen seconds using forked sticks to straddle a barrier consisting of an eight-foot-high game fence and razor wire stacked three layers high. The South Africa Defense Forces estimate that they catch only one person in four who crosses, and even these will try again until they succeed—one person was caught twenty-eight times in six months.[18] No one knows how many undocumented immigrants are in South Africa: estimates vary from 2.5 million to 8 million (one-tenth of the population). These are largely guesswork, but the figures on expulsions are more solid: in 1990, the year Nelson Mandela was freed, 53,418 people were expelled. In 1995, the first full year of democratic rule, South Africa expelled 157,084 people, mostly to Mozambique.[19]

Economic Disruption

While modernization and capitalist development in general have always been disruptive, a number of recent processes integral to globalization have intensified the effects. The sequence of events since 1973 onwards has shaken the economies of many countries. After the first oil shock, the recession in industrial countries, along with the sharp rise in oil prices, hit many developing countries hard. Between 1972 and 1981, the debts of developing countries rose from less than $100 billion to more than $600 billion.[20]

The struggle to resolve the debt crisis drew many countries into an uncomfortably close relationship with the IMF and the World Bank. The World Bank gave loans to most countries in Latin America and sub-Saharan Africa on the strict condition that they restructure their economies along free-market lines. These measures had a profound impact, often negative, on employment and livelihoods. The lowering of trade barriers, for example, exposed both agriculture and industry to the cold winds of international competition, often reducing employment and wages. Cuts in government expenditure reduced public-sector employment and curtailed many vital social services and subsidies on which the poor depended.

The experience of the developing countries was far from uniform, however, and the impact on employment, and the implications for migration, are easier to relate in regional terms.

Latin America and the Caribbean. The economic collapse of the early 1980s wiped out many gains of earlier decades. Between 1980 and 1990, per capita GDP fell by 9.6 percent and consumption by 6 percent.[21] As formal employment opportunities declined, so more people moved to the informal sector: between 1980 and 1992 the proportion of those in nonagricultural work who gained their livelihoods in the informal sector rose from 25 percent to 32 percent.[22] This brought total underutilization of the labor force (unemployment plus underemployment) to 42 percent. At the same time, wages in the region were falling. The decline varied across sectors, ranging from 5 percent in industry to 20 percent in agriculture. In the informal sector, average wages declined even more sharply—by 42 percent.[23] Unsurprisingly, the 1980s were regarded as a "lost decade" in Latin America. Since then there have been signs of recovery. Most countries have achieved greater macroeconomic stability and growth rates of over 3 percent. But this has yet to translate into significant improvements in employment and income.[24]

Sub-Saharan Africa. The recession after the oil shock had a disastrous effect on livelihoods in sub-Saharan Africa, the only region of the world where standards of living have been on a steady downward path. Since 1973, per capita output has declined by 10 percent. Over the past two decades, total agricultural income has dropped by 15 percent, and encouraged 6 to 8 percent of the population to leave the countryside each year for the cities. This has compounded the already deteriorating position in urban areas—in both formal and informal sectors. Urban unemployment, which was around 10 percent in the mid-1970s, now ranges between 15 percent and 20 percent. The informal sector in most African towns and cities became the employer of last resort—and is now believed to employ over 60 percent of the urban labor force.

South Asia. The countries of South Asia avoided the extreme experiences of Latin America and Africa. Less exposed to international financial and commodity markets, they largely missed the debt crisis of the 1980s. Most employment is in agriculture, and increases in production as a result of the green revolution helped absorb much of the increase in the labor force. Industrialization in South Asia had been based on import substitution, which increased output, but not very efficiently, and without absorbing much of the urban labor force. Manufacturing employment during the 1980s grew at less than 1 percent per year. As elsewhere, the burden has been passed to the informal sector, which in India and Pakistan in 1990 accounted for over 70 percent of total manufacturing employment.

North Africa and the Middle East. This is a very heterogeneous group, including rich oil exporters and labor importers in the Persian Gulf, as well as poorer labor exporters such as Egypt and Yemen. Most of these countries gained from the oil price rises, either as oil exporters or through remittances from migrant workers. The fall in oil prices in the mid-1980s provoked something of a crisis in the region, and since then a number of countries have undertaken adjustment programs. In most countries, unemployment was around 7 percent in the 1970s but in the post-recession period it is now 10 percent or more.[25]

East and Southeast Asia. Until recently, this was the world's fastest-growing region, and growth was transmitted very effectively into employment. In 1990, only 15 percent of the region's population lived below the poverty line—compared with 28 percent in Latin America and the Caribbean. This is not just because of economic growth, but also because of much greater equality.[26] China has followed a somewhat different path. Its steady progression toward a market economy has been accompanied by a further boost in economic growth. Inequality has certainly increased, but most people in China are better off, and the number of people living in absolute poverty has fallen steeply over the last two decades. By 1998, however, the future was looking much less certain and economic disruption—if it persists—could eventually start to dislodge many people who thought their futures would be at home.

The pressures of recession and structural adjustment have thus had diverse impacts around the world. Nevertheless, the general effect has been a crisis of economic security. People moving from the rural areas to the cities find that they have to take two or three jobs in the informal sector to survive. It is just this lack of security that drives many individuals to migrate overseas.

However, in many cases this is not an individual decision. Most emigrants are playing their part in a family survival strategy. Thus a rural family might spread its risks by having some family members work in agriculture but send others to work in the city or overseas as a way of spreading the risks of failure. The emigrant thus takes out a kind of "co-insurance" with the rest of the family. The head of the family will pay the emigrant's initial expenses of travel and subsistence while he or she is looking for work, and the emigrant promises to send regular remittances—increasing them at times when the family at home is in particular difficulty.[27] One form of this system has been observed in families divided across the U.S.-Mexico border. Those who work in the United States tend to be young or middle-aged men, who can earn higher wages—though the risks and the costs of unemployment are high. Meanwhile those under eighteen, the women, and the old stay in Mexico, where wages might be low but there is greater security and fewer out-of-pocket expenses.[28]

Social Disruption

Beyond unsettling people who lose their jobs, globalization is also altering the character of society. This can be seen partly as a continuation of the process of modernization, as traditional communities and extended families give way to nuclear families, and as subsistence economies are penetrated by capitalism and consumer culture.

Globalization has certainly intensified this process of opening up and atomizing communities—and is challenging people in every society to see themselves in relation not just to their immediate neighbors but to the rest of the world. This is evident in the spread of global media. Even in the least-developed countries, there is now approximately one radio for every ten people, and one television set for every hundred.[29] Within the urban areas that are the stepping-off points for most emigrants, the proportions are much higher—even the most miserable slums in Latin America usually display a forest of television antennae. Added to these are myriad other forms of communication—from cinema, to magazines, to popular music.

Much of this material is imported. Every country has twenty-four hours in the day, and each national television broadcaster tries to fill up the airtime. The cheapest way to do this is by buying in programs from abroad. Similarly, the most spectacular movies will generally come from wealthier parts of the world. China is only the latest country to find itself swamped by the products of Hollywood: Chinese moviegoers are increasingly ignoring government-produced films and, despite official disapproval, are flocking to see the latest movies from Hong Kong (China) or the United States. Added to this is the information beamed in directly by satellite. At the end of 1996, there were an estimated seven hundred live satellites orbiting the earth.[30]

Nevertheless, the flows are becoming increasingly dispersed. UNESCO has looked at the sources of the trade in cultural goods of all kinds—from literature, to television, to music. It found that the share of industrial countries dropped between 1975 and 1990 from over 90 to less than 70 percent.[31] American television may still have the biggest audiences, but movies from India and Hong Kong (China), soap operas from Mexico and Argentina, and pop music from Africa are finding a worldwide audience. This is not to say that people will inevitably prefer the foreign product. When a choice exists, well-produced local programs tend to score higher in the ratings. Nevertheless, people are getting the option to judge their culture in relation to foreign alternatives. Of migrant-sending countries, the Philippines is probably the most penetrated by foreign, almost entirely U.S., media. A 1994 report on television patterns found that foreign programs made up 32 percent of airtime and accounted for 37 percent of programs watched.[32]

Beyond the penetration of foreign media, there is also the distribution of products that contribute to a sense of belonging to a global consumer culture. The leading global brand in 1996 was judged to be McDonald's, with 19,000 hamburger restaurants scattered around the world, followed by Coca-Cola, Disney, Kodak, and Sony.[33] Just as much as the consular offices of migrant-receiving countries, the global brands serve as focal points of a new and increasingly hybrid consumption culture. Again, McDonald's is normally considered the archetype of imposed uniformity. In Egypt, for example, it has been pointed out that almost all the menu items, even "apple pie" and "milk shake" are not even translated but merely transliterated into Arabic.[34]

However, such companies do not necessarily displace local alternatives, and not all come from industrial countries. A number of fast-food chains such as the Philippines company Jollibee have their origins in other developing countries, and advertising developed in one country may soon be seen elsewhere. One highly successful campaign for Nescafé, for example, originated in Chile and in 1996 was being seen in many other countries.[35] Some would argue that all this has made the world a more peaceful place. At the end of 1996, the *New York Times* was able to report that no two countries with a branch of McDonald's had ever gone to war against each other.[36]

The increasing complexity of the global cultural environment has led sociologist Arju Appadurai to suggest that it can best be understood through a new series of "scapes." The "Ethnoscape" is the landscape of people—tourists, immigrants, refugees, and others who move around the world affecting the countries where they arrive. The "Technoscape" is the fluid configuration of technology that allows products in one place to arrive from almost anywhere—a steel plant in the Libyan Arab Jamahariya, for example, might involve interests from India, China, Russia, and Japan. The "Finanscape" consists of the flood of capital that rushes at breathtaking speed through international networks. The "Mediascape" refers both to multinational media distribution networks and to the images they portray, which through complex narratives and mixtures are creating new "imagined worlds." The "Ideoscape" consists of ideologies and counterideologies and ideas such as "freedom," "welfare," and "rights." Appadurai argues that modern culture is increasingly shaped by the growing disjuncture between all these "scapes."[37]

One of the most important disjunctions is to draw people into the cash economy—and yet offer them little by way of reward. In Mexico, for example, Mixtec Indians are increasingly being drawn out of their own areas in the south to employment on huge farms in the north that export cash crops to the United States. They go to Sinaloa to work on winter vegetable production and to Baja California to grow tomatoes and other vegetables. Once there, and earning money, it soon becomes clear that they could do better by venturing further north. One survey found that 77 percent of Mixtecs in California and Oregon had previously worked either in Baja or Sinaloa, or both, before migrating to the United States. After people had moved from remote rural areas, they were exposed to networks of contacts that opened up a new range of possibilities—especially since work in both places was much the same, making it easier for the migrants to find employment.[38]

Another important reason that deeper involvement in the cash economy can encourage migration is that it allows people to pay the costs of emigration. Even so, they will still have to save up. North Africans in Morocco, who might be earning around $4 per day, would have to work the best part of a year to be able to afford the perilous ten-mile crossing from Tangier to Tarifa on the southern tip of Spain. In 1996 this illegal trip cost $600. Even legal migration is very expensive. In the Philippines, recruiters are officially permitted to charge migrants around $200, but in fact charge up to $4,000 for jobs in Japan or Taiwan (China). South Asian and Chinese migrants to the United States have been charged much more. A group of immigrants apprehended in 1996 told officials that they had paid a $28,000 fee in three disbursements made to handlers in Asia, Nicaragua, and Mexico—having been lodged along the way at safe houses in Moscow, Havana, Managua, Guatemala, and Mexico City.

Many migrants do not pay up front. Rural families frequently borrow at exorbitant interest rates to finance emigration. In other cases, recruiters and contractors often find it more profitable to take money out of the migrants' future earnings—even keeping them locked up in workplaces to ensure that they do not escape. Nevertheless, the process of economic development that enables emigrants to save up at least a part of the cost is an important contribution toward emigration.

The Migration Hump

The disturbing effect of development—shaking people loose from their communities, raising new possibilities, and providing them with the funds to travel—means that as countries achieve a minimum standard of economic development, then migration is likely to increase rather than decrease.

This can be expressed graphically as a "migration hump," as emigration first rises as GDP per capita rises, but after a while starts to fall again.[39] On the basis of emigration patterns in southern Europe from the 1960s to the 1980s, the GDP per capita turning point for a sample of countries was estimated to average $3,615—ranging from $3,400 for Turkey to $4,100 for Greece (in 1985 international dollar prices).[40]

However, it has also been suggested that the watershed level is different depending on the level of skill of the potential migrant and the cost and distance of migration. This is illustrated in Figure 7.1, which shows the stylized phases of mobility patterns.

Conclusion

For almost everyone caught up in the modern phase of globalization, one of the most significant effects has been an increase in uncertainty.

Figure 7.1   The Migration Hump

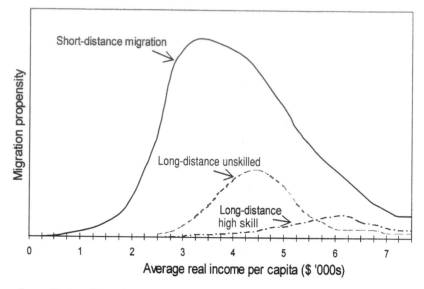

Source: Fischer, P., and T. Straubhaar, 1996.

With communities all over the world more closely interlinked, the global economic environment has become steadily more dynamic—and in many respects more unstable—as competition intensifies and economic shocks are transmitted instantly around the globe. Among those most sharply affected by this new environment are people in the poorest countries who find themselves drawn ever further into a global economy. In the short term, even if the poor benefit from these links, this will probably make them more prone to emigrate—though in the long term the same processes could provide them with greater incentives to stay at home.

Notes

1. Massey, D. 1988, p. 383.
2. Alburo, F. A. 1994, p. 50.
3. UNFPA. 1993, p. 11.
4. United Nations. 1994.
5. Camp, S. 1990.
6. Stalker, P. 1997, p. 6.
7. Gilbert, A. 1994, p. 22.
8. Massey, D. 1988, p. 383.
9. UNDP. 1996, p. 23.

10. Bennett Jones, O. 1996.
11. Atkinson, R. 1996.
12. *Migration News,* vol. 3, no. 9.
13. *Economist.* 1995e.
14. Iglebaek, O. 1995.
15. Brzezinski, M. 1995.
16. Hopper, J. 1995.
17. UNDP. 1996, p. 22.
18. Minnaar, A., et al. 1995.
19. Drogin, B. 1996.
20. UNRISD. 1995, p. 32.
21. ILO. 1992, p. 44.
22. ILO. 1994, p. 18.
23. ILO. 1995, p. 66.
24. ILO. 1994, p. 18.
25. Khan, A. 1994, p. 62.
26. ILO. 1995, p. 64.
27. Stark, O. 1992, p. 32.
28. Zabin, C., and S. Hughes. 1995, p. 412.
29. UNDP. 1996, p. 167.
30. Stansell, J. 1996.
31. World Commission on Culture and Development. 1995, p. 27.
32. UNESCO. 1994, p. 79.
33. Kochan, N. 1996, p. 83.
34. Peterson, M. 1998, p. 122.
35. Wentsz, L. 1996, p. 121.
36. Friedman, T. 1996.
37. Appadurai, A. 1990, p. 295.
38. Zabin, C., and S. Hughes. 1995, p. 415.
39. Martin, P., and J. Taylor. 1996, p. 43.
40. Faini, R., and A. Venturini. 1994, p. 15.

8

The International Skill Exchange

Worries about international migration generally focus on unskilled workers. Skilled workers or professionals are regarded in quite a different light. Indeed, most countries have been happy to accept, or go out of their way to attract, such people. Globalization is adding to this cadre and giving them more opportunities to capitalize on their skills by moving to a new employer or, if they are employees of transnational corporations, by transferring between affiliates.

The Brain Drain

Most professionals travel between rich countries, or from poor countries to rich, and, as with unskilled workers, the main motivation for professional migrants will be to increase their income.[1] In 1991, a staff nurse in Manila would get only $146 per month, while she or he could earn around $500 in the Persian Gulf and $3,000 in the United States.[2] As a result, the Philippines in recent decades has been exporting nurses at a rate of 3,000 or more per year.[3] But migration of professionals is prompted not only by salary differentials but also by the opportunities to develop their careers and keep abreast of their chosen field of knowledge.

While it may be advantageous for the individuals, this "brain drain" represents a considerable loss to countries that have invested in workers' training and skill. Today, it is thought that there are about one and a half million skilled expatriates from developing countries in Western Europe, the United States, Japan, and Australia. Africa has probably been worst hit. Between 1985 and 1990, it is said to have lost 60,000 professionals and to have been losing 20,000 per year ever since.[4] Ghana, for example, lost 60 percent of doctors trained in the early 1980s. In recent years, Eastern European countries have been facing the same problems. Bulgaria has been one of the countries hardest hit. In 1995, it lost more than 7,000 professors and researchers. This is not too surprising, because they had been earning only around $50 per month. One survey in 1996 found that 40 percent of Bulgaria's scientists were planning to emigrate.[5]

Migration of professionals is often driven by considerations of personal or professional advancement, but it is also facilitated by the policies of receiving countries—which skew their immigration systems in favor of professional immigrants. Canada, for example, has had a very methodical system that awards points for education and skill. It also admits virtually anyone who will invest at least $250,000 in a Canadian business. Of the 205,000 planned admissions for 1997, up to 113,000 were to come under the skilled or business categories.[6] Australia, too, has been moving more in this direction—under the migration program for 1998–1999 more than half were to come under the "skill stream."[7]

The United States has also been trying to increase the proportion of immigrants who are skilled—though it has had rather less success. Indeed, many people have expressed concern about educational qualifications of immigrants to the United States in general. This is usually gauged in terms of their earnings relative to the rest of the population. Between 1970 and 1990, average earnings of immigrant men fell from 99 to 89 percent of those of national workers. However, there were considerable disparities between national groups. Europeans and Canadians held their own, with wages 10 to 20 percent higher than nationals. Chinese, Japanese, and Korean immigrants have actually seen their relative earnings rise—from 88 to 110 percent. Most of the fall results from the large numbers of Mexicans whose earnings fell on average from 66 to 56 percent.[8]

Moreover, in recent years the U.S. visa category corresponding to skilled workers—the employment visa—has not been filled. Between 1993 and 1995, the number of employment-based visas dropped from 147,000 to 85,000 and currently represents only 12 percent of legal immigrants. Nowadays, more than half of these come from Asia: China alone provided 16 percent of employment-based immigrants, followed by the Philippines (12 percent) and India (8 percent).[9]

The Globalization of Education

The flow of professionals around the world has been intensified by the globalization of higher education. In 1993 an estimated 1.5 million students were studying overeas.[10] The highest numbers are coming from Asia—and most of these are heading for the United States. Between the mid-1950s and the mid-1980s, the number of overseas students from South and East Asia increased from 10,000 to over 140,000.[11] In 1990, 62 percent of engineering doctorates in the United States were given to foreign students, mainly Asian. The proportion was almost as high in a number of other fields, such as mathematics, computer science, and the physical sciences.

Many of these professionals head for richer countries after completing training at home, but others are lost when they fail to return after completing their studies overseas. One estimate is that over 70 percent of foreign-born Ph.D.'s remain in the United States, many of them becoming citizens.[12] Chinese officials said in 1995 that of the 220,000 Chinese students who had gone abroad since 1979, only 75,000 had returned.[13]

Transnational Employers

The majority of professionals travel under their own steam, but some are also being transferred within transnational corporations—from one affiliate to another. Most transnationals now employ relatively few expatriates. For U.S. transnationals for whom figures were available in 1989, expatriates accounted for only 0.3 percent of total employment in foreign affiliates—mostly concentrated in senior management positions. The proportion tends to be higher for affiliates in developing countries. For a sample of U.S. companies in the late 1980s, while 10 percent of European affiliates had expatriate senior management, the figure for Latin American affiliates was 53 percent.[14] However, the proportion tends to be very high when affiliates are being established—as is currently happening on a vast scale in China, where in 1995 there were an estimated 450,000 expatriate managers.[15]

The proportion of expatriates tends to be higher for Japanese companies—but still only 4 percent of total employment in their foreign affiliates. Again, the proportion is much higher for senior management. A sample of employees in Japanese companies found that senior management was 77 percent expatriate in European affiliates but 83 percent in Latin American affiliates. The higher proportion for Japanese management may be due to communications concerns—with the need for top management to be in touch with the home country. This is partly a matter of language because Japanese is not widely spoken outside Japan, but also because the management style of Japanese companies is based more on informal networks.[16]

The Republic of Korea, the latest addition to the list of TNC host countries, still has a fairly shallow pool of international experience on which to draw. At times this has caused labor relations problems. In China, for example, a Korean supervisor in Qingdao had rocks thrown through his windows after he explained to local staff that Koreans "overcame poverty with hard work and discipline." In Indonesia, the alleged mistreatment of workers by Korean managers has sparked strikes and labor unrest. Korean companies investing in Europe are therefore making a greater effort to recruit local managers. Samsung Electronics, for example, has recruited British managers for its home-appliance factory in northeast England.[17]

Originally, expatriate staff were needed to exert control over affiliates and also to meet gaps in skills that were not available locally. Later these objectives seem to have been widened, in attempts to build a more "internationalized" cadre of management capable of operating in many different countries. Frequently, this has meant employing "third-country" nationals—around 7 percent of the senior management of affiliates of U.S. companies consists of third-country nationals.

Expatriate employment is unlikely to rise greatly in the years ahead and certainly not in proportion to the rise in foreign direct investment. The main reason is cost. Pay for expatriates is high: apart from a premium of 10–20 percent of base salary, there are numerous allowances for housing and schooling, as well as the expense of relocation. It might cost double the regular base salary to employ someone overseas. A recent estimate suggests that the average net overseas cost per executive was $131,000. For the United Kingdom alone, which annually has around 48,000 corporate transferees, this suggests that TNCs are spending about $6.3 billion per year moving their highly skilled staff in and out of the country.[18] In any case, technology is now offering cheaper ways of keeping an eye on affiliates. Increasingly effective systems of communication—from e-mail to video conferencing—are reducing the need for physical presence. In 1995, the managers at Daimler-Benz's new factory in Alabama, for example, were holding daily two-hour teleconferences with the head office in Stuttgart.[19]

Local Professionals

Beyond cost, employing host-country nationals offers considerable advantages because they are more likely to be familiar with the language and customs—and can deal better with local officials and exploit market opportunities. U.S. companies in Malaysia, for example, have been making determined efforts to employ Malaysians. In 1991, of the 180 U.S. companies with registered offices in the country, 66 had Malaysian managing directors and the process seems to have accelerated since then.[20]

As educational standards rise around the world, employing local people also permits companies to make better use of local talent. Citibank, for example, uses workers in India, Hong Kong (China), and Singapore to develop financial services for use globally. Hewlett-Packard also has moved on rapidly from employing cheap labor in affiliates to using them for advanced R&D. In Singapore, a plant the company opened in 1970 to assemble keyboards is now the global R&D and production center for portable ink-jet printers, as well as being the base for personal digital assistants and calculators. Cost is also a significant incentive. In the United States, skilled electronics engineers in 1994 could earn up to $100,000 per year, while in Taiwan (China) they were available for $25,000, and in India or China for less than $10,000.[21]

The Reverse Brain Drain

So keen are TNCs to employ people with local language skills or knowledge that they are stimulating a reverse brain drain—tempting people who have migrated to industrial countries to move to developing countries. The United States, as a major immigration destination, has the advantage here, since it has a large pool of cross-cultural personnel on which to draw. A survey of U.S. TNCs in Taiwan (China) found that no less than 35 percent of expatriate staff were of Chinese extraction. Many of these had gone to the United States from Taiwan (China) as students, stayed on to work, and become naturalized citizens. Later they were recruited by TNCs and sent back to the territory. Others might be called "quasi-expatriates"—students from Taiwan (China) recruited while still on U.S. campuses. After gaining experience in the territory, such people may then be sent on to mainland China.[22] However, U.S. companies can also make good use of the offspring of immigrants, who usually speak some Chinese.

These American-born Chinese (ABCs) are now in high demand in Hong Kong (China) and China generally. For many this is a way of breaking through the "glass ceiling" that in the United States tends to keep them in technical rather than managerial jobs. Even through the Asian financial crisis the demand continued to be strong.[23] European countries with fewer Asian immigrants and students do not have many of these options, and most of their TNC expatriates are European.

Return Migration

For many of the ethnic Chinese recruited to work for TNCs in Asia, this amounts to "return migration." But independent return migration is now taking place on quite a significant scale. For all U.S. immigrants, it has been estimated that as many as 20 percent leave the United States within ten years of arrival, and one-third leave again over their lifetime.[24] In the mid-1990s, around 200,000 foreign-born Americans were leaving each year. Not all of these people are professionals, but in the mid-1990s previous immigrants from a number of Asian countries were returning to take advantage of the new prosperity—particularly in the Republic of Korea and Taiwan (China).

The Republic of Korea was long a country of emigration. Between 1970 and 1990, some 750,000 people left the country—the annual figure peaked in 1976 at 46,533, and by 1994 had tailed off to 14,604. Some people are still emigrating, but the balance has shifted dramatically. During the peak years, Korean emigrants outnumbered returnees by a 19 to 1 ratio. In 1994, it was only about 2 to 1.[25]

In some cases, people have been leaving the United States during periods of economic downturn. Some Koreans who have found the English language difficult have faced racial discrimination and are worried about violence and crime. But the Republic of Korea, at least prior to the Asian financial crisis, was proving more attractive— and visibly so (the numbers of those returning increased sharply after the 1988 Seoul Olympics). Many of those who went to the United States and opened grocery stores and delicatessens, for example, find it hard to keep going, and those professionals who had to downgrade their skills to become shopkeepers find returning particularly attractive—especially those with English language skills. A professor at Cornell University who became chair of the life sciences department at a Korean university staffed his entire department with Korean-American professors.[26] In order to take advantage of similar pools of talent, the government is planning to recruit more ethnic Koreans as teachers, lawyers, and scientists.

In Taiwan (China) this reverse flow is called the *rencai huiliu*— the "return flow of human talent." Many are being attracted back to aerospace and other industries in the high-technology city of Hsinchu. Even if this means taking a pay cut of 30 to 40 percent, they seem happy to make the move, seeing the prospect of a better future in Taiwan (China). The transition is not always smooth. Those who have adopted America's more freewheeling attitudes in business, with robust give-and-take between executives at all levels, face readaptation to the more sedate Chinese ways of doing business. There can also be resentment at returnees taking the best jobs. But despite the recent economic downturn, more and more former emigrants are concluding that the future lies with Asia.[27]

The New Skill Exchange

Apart from expatriates brought in by TNCs, Asia's rapid development in the 1980s and early 1990s also brought in non-Asians. Many young people from Western countries who have had difficulty finding work at home discovered better prospects in Asia. Hong Kong (China) in the years leading up to 1997 proved a particular magnet. These were not all the traditionally highly paid expatriates, but a more heterogeneous mixture: some worked in pizza parlors or as domestic servants—known locally as "FILTH" (Failed In London, Try Hong Kong)—and were employed at local wages. In Singapore, young European graduates recruited to work in the financial-services sector were employed at local wages. In Malaysia, young out-of-work British architects were employed in the construction industry. There is also a more even playing field when it comes to promotion—with companies now much more keen on encouraging local talent.

Westerners have not just been heading for Asia. Young business graduates are increasingly choosing a wider range of destinations. The other target areas tend to be Eastern Europe and Latin America (especially Mexico in the wake of NAFTA). Some estimates suggest that the number of young Americans heading abroad increased by between 10 and 25 percent in the early 1990s. At Stanford Business School, 14 percent of the class of 1994 elected to seek jobs abroad, compared with 6 percent in 1989.[28]

At the same time, there is also a much more diverse pool of talent swirling around between developing countries. Again, Asia is the focus of much of this—with demand for technical and professional staff regularly outstripping supply. Chinese Malaysians, for example, with fluency in both Chinese and English, are in great demand. Many Malaysians are working on short-term contracts for banks and other companies in Indonesia. Singaporeans can be found working here too, as well as in Hong Kong (China), Taiwan (China), and southern China. Filipino professionals are also moving around the region. Accountants are particularly sought after—Filipinos occupy key positions in Indonesia's top commercial banks. Even Japanese managers, faced for the first time with redundancy at home, have started to head for other Asian countries.

In a further twist to the story, some of these professionals are also being drawn on a contract basis to the United States, where they can undercut local wage rates. This is particularly evident in the computer industry. In 1995, a large New York insurance company, for example, laid off 250 computer programmers and replaced them with lower-wage temporary workers from India. Even the White House has resorted to cheap technical help, using a company that imports most of its workers from India to upgrade the president's correspondence-tracking computer system. Each year, tens of thousands of such workers from around the world are brought into the United States under the H-1B visa program, which admits computer programmers, engineers, scientists, health-care workers, and others under nonimmigrant status. Many are imported by job-contracting firms known as "body shops," which recruit foreign professionals and hire them out to major U.S. companies. Critics of the program describe these imported professionals, who are effectively indentured to their employers, as "techno-*braceros*," the high-tech equivalent of migrant farm workers.[29]

Conclusion

As globalization proceeds, the flows of professionals may not increase in volume, but are likely to become ever more complex. At present, there is relatively little resistance to these flows, since so far they have largely filled gaps at the top of the employment ladder. But with employment agencies developing cadres of mobile, educated, and skilled people that can be employed on short-term contracts, there could be a stronger response from local professionals who feel they are being undercut by cheaper foreign-based workers.

Notes

1. Ong, P., L. Cheng, and L. Evans. 1992, p. 557.
2. *Asiaweek.* 1991.
3. World Bank. 1993, p. 141.
4. *ACP-EU Courier.* 1996, p. 59.
5. *Migration News,* vol. 4, no. 1.
6. Citizenship and Immigration Canada. 1997.
7. Department of Immigration and Multicultural Affairs. 1998.
8. Vernez, G., and K. McCarthy. 1996.
9. U.S. Immigration and Naturalization Service. 1996.
10. Salt, J., and J. Stein. 1997, p. 469.
11. Ong, P., L. Cheng, and L. Evans. 1992, p. 557.
12. Bhagwati, J., and M. Rao. 1996, p. 50.
13. *Migration News,* vol. 2, no. 5.
14. UNCTAD. 1994, p. 238.
15. *Economist.* 1995c.

16. UNCTAD. 1994, p. 239.
17. Hoon, S. J. 1995.
18. Salt, J. 1996, p. 86.
19. *Economist.* 1995d, p. 25.
20. Vatikiotis, M. 1994.
21. Engardio, P. 1994.
22. Tzeng, R. 1995, p. 139.
23. Miller, M. 1998.
24. Bratsberg, B., and D. Terrell. 1996, p. 789.
25. Kim, J-Y. 1995.
26. Belluck, P. 1995.
27. Dunn, A. 1995.
28. Gray, P. 1994.
29. Branigan, W. 1995.

9

Lubricating the Flow

As Adam Smith observed, "a man is of all sorts of luggage the most difficult to be transported."[1] That is as true today as ever, though the nature of the difficulty has changed. Today the major hurdle is likely to be political. Governments in industrial countries are more protective of national frontiers and are determined to keep out those people they believe might cause economic, social, or political problems. Nevertheless, a number of other developments in recent years have encouraged the flow of migrants—particularly the expansion in global communications and transport, and the development of an international migration industry.

Messages from the Media

Thanks largely to television, most potential emigrants will have attractive images of the wealth of their destination countries. These media flows have no direct connection with migrant flows, but they nevertheless sustain the idea of an increasingly globalized society. Indeed, it can be argued that we are moving toward a "global culture." At its simplest, this raises the prospect of greater wealth elsewhere. Spanish television channels carrying game shows, for example, can be picked up in some parts of North Africa. As one Civil Guard commander has commented, "They see that and they think Spain is a paradise."[2] But at a more general level, the flow of news and multinational dramas creates the impression that it does not much matter where you live—you could be at home anywhere.

This idea is sustained when immigrants arrive and are welcomed into the arms of the new ethnic media. Most sizeable immigrant communities have their own newspapers and even television stations. Vancouver, for example, has one of the fastest-growing Chinese-speaking communities in the world and now has three Chinese daily news-papers, three mainly Chinese radio stations, and two television sta-tions.[3] These media are good sources of news from the home coun-try—and of international news in general. In the United States, the huge Hispanic community is well served by Spanish-language TV sta-tions. As Federico Subervi of the University of Texas puts it, the Spanish-language networks along with the Spanish language itself are the "glue of Latino identity across the country."[4]

Specifically on immigration issues, these media offer a different perspective to the rest of the press and television. In the United States in 1993, for example, when the attorney-general was found to have employed an undocumented immigrant as a nanny, the English-language newspapers used this as an opportunity to explore the plight of middle-class women who wanted to go out to work. The Spanish-language media, however, sought out Hispanic women work-ing as housekeepers and nannies and published their stories of abuse and exploitation.

These stations are also increasingly important as sources of infor-mation about the United States for Latin America. Univisión or its com-petitor Telemundo are available on almost all cable systems in Latin America. In poorer countries, smaller television stations often tape items from their U.S. bulletins for use in their own news programs.

Telecommunications and Transportation

The mass media represent one part of the global flow of information that eases the passage of immigrants. Just as important in reducing the emotional distance between one country and another has been the rapid increase in, and declining costs of, global communications. In 1994, international telephone traffic amounted to some 53 billion minutes—up threefold over the previous decade.[5] While this expan-sion has been driven by the demands of global business, migrants have been able to take advantage of opportunities to keep in touch with their home communities. Indeed, they often do so at various stages along the route. This is easier for those with families in urban areas because developing countries lag far behind the industrial ones in telephone connections. Even in relatively advanced countries such as Chile and Thailand, in 1995 more than half the telephone lines were in the capital city. But the gaps are rapidly narrowing, with satellite communications and mobile telephony helping the coun-tries with weaker infrastructure to leapfrog a communications gen-eration. In the Philippines in 1996, for example, for every thousand people there were only twenty-five mainline telephones but thirteen mobile phones.[6]

Telephone companies have not been slow to exploit the immigrant market. In the United States, long-distance carriers make a point of mailing promotional material to new arrivals and offering special rates to each community for their national holidays. In Japan, immigrants can be seen clustered around public telephones queuing to make their calls home. In Tel Aviv, in the many shops advertising cut-rate telephone services, clocks display the local time in India, Ecuador, and the Philippines.

According to one investigator in El Salvador, the main social gathering place in any town is no longer the church or the plaza, and the most important people are no longer the priest or the mayor. The center of social activity now is Antel (the local telephone office), and the key people are telephone operators who are gatekeepers to contact with the United States. The Antel operator in San José de la Paz Arriba, a town of 3,000, places 350 to 400 calls to the United States each month, all of them "collect" or "reverse charge," calls to be paid by the receiver—and lasting twenty to ninety minutes.[7]

Communication is not limited to the telephone. One Guatemalan group in Houston, for example, reportedly used faxes to organize an elaborate birthday celebration for a family member in their hometown of San Cristóbal Totonicapán. Among other things, the fax traffic was used to recruit participants, select traditional motifs, and schedule payments for ceremonial materials and food supplies.[8]

At an even higher level of sophistication, for immigrants with access to the Internet there is also an increasing number of web sites. The immigration services of all major receiving countries now have sites offering the latest information and regulations. There are also sites that enable cultural connections between members of different ethnic groups. In the United States, more than two hundred "immigration lawyers" also have their own web sites.

Another communications development is the steep drop in the costs of transportation. This enabled international travel and tourism to more than double between 1980 and 1996, and barriers to migration have been greatly lowered. Many migrants enter the richer countries as tourists and overstay their visas. Until a few years ago, for example, immigrants to Japan from many poor countries, including Pakistan and Bangladesh, did not even need visas. Any capital city in the world is now only hours away from Tokyo or Paris. Even for an unskilled worker, the expense of flying represents no more than a month's earnings in an industrial country.

Migrant Networks

The increased scale and diversity of global communications systems have certainly made international migration easier. But just as important as communications networks are the human networks—the links between sending and receiving countries established by previous generations of migrants. Relatively few migrants, documented or otherwise, will travel without some contacts in their destination country—people who can arrange for compatriots everything from employment to housing. One of the most important functions of the network is to provide information. Regular home visits, as well as telephone calls, keep home communities abreast of the latest situation. A study of Filipino immigrants to the United States in the mid-1980s, for example, found that the primary source of information about visas, and all the other immigration procedures, was not the embassy or travel agents but personal contacts.[9]

These networks can also be crucial for getting a legal visa. Most countries have been tightening up on immigration and reducing the entry channels so that, for many people, joining other family members is virtually the only way of getting in legally. In the United States in 1996, family reunification accounted for 65 percent of immigration, and in Australia the 1998–1999 immigration plan assumed that 45 percent of immigrants would come in as family members. Family reunification is also one of the most significant categories in Europe—accounting for one-third of immigration to the United Kingdom, for example.

The presence of family members is also a temptation for undocumented immigration. Though Turkish labor immigration to the Netherlands has now halted, many people continue to enter as tourists in the hope that relatives will be able to find them a job. The high proportion of family immigrants is one of the main reasons for the rapid change in the ethnic balance of immigrants—some nationalities have a greater enthusiasm for bringing in family members than others. In the United States, for example, settled immigrants from Asia are more likely to sponsor relatives than are immigrants from Europe.[10]

Links with family and friends are also of primary importance when settling in new communities. Most immigrants nowadays will have somewhere to stay when they arrive. A 1990 study of Brazilian immigrants to Canada asked where they stayed when they first arrived. It found that 39 percent stayed with friends who were already in Canada, while a further 20 percent stayed with relatives.[11]

But human networks are probably of greatest value when it comes to finding work. Once immigrants become established in a particular worksite or location, they generate further job opportunities for those who follow. These human chains often start with one person. Thus in the mid-1980s when an immigrant from Santiago in the Mexican state of Jalisco became a union representative in a lamp factory in Los Angeles, he then drew many other people from the same town. A similar set of links have been established between the town of Gómez Farías and the strawberry fields in Watsonville, California: around 90 percent of migrants from Gómez Farías work there because early arrivals had developed connections with particular growers.[12] Interestingly, the same kinds of links are also evident for migration *into* Mexico. Coffee cultivation in the southern state of Chiapas, for example, is heavily dependent on families migrating in for six to eight months from the western highlands of Guatemala. Employees typically work at the same place each year and pass the relationship along to friends and relatives.[13] Equivalent links have been established between communities in many other countries. In Germany, for example, investigators found a cluster of several hundred Turkish villagers from East Anatolia and the Black Sea coast living and working closely together in Berlin.[14]

In certain cases, these unofficial employment exchanges have become so powerful that immigrant communities now dominate employment niches. This is noticeable in the United States where many jobs that might equally well be filled by unskilled U.S. employees have been taken over by Latino immigrants. Hotels and restaurants in Los Angeles, for example, recruit a high proportion of their staff through referrals from other employees. As a result, kitchen worker jobs are often filled by close-knit groups of Mexican workers. Employers are happy with this arrangement because it is an efficient way of providing staff who have the right qualifications for the work, and it also ensures better performance since recruiters are under pressure to make sure their protégés perform.[15] But the same is often true even in larger enterprises. In 1990, Mexican immigrants were heavily overrepresented in fifty-three of Los Angeles' eighty largest manufacturing industries. Immigrant workers know which of their friends is thinking of leaving, so they will actually be aware of potential vacancies before the employer. A supervisor in a printing plant quoted in the *New York Times* said: "The referrals occur before the vacancy appears. Everybody out there knows about it before we do."[16]

Most investigations of employment through immigrant networks have concerned men. But many of the same processes apply to women. A study of Filipino women in Hawaii, for example, found that women tended to find their first jobs through relatives and friends. In some cases, these would provide contacts at private employment agencies—and even offer informal training. However, one of the difficulties for women immigrants is that networks tend to concentrate on low-level "women's" jobs. As a result, women who might have been secretaries or teachers in their home countries find themselves taking low-wage service jobs as domestic workers or as nurses' aides.[17]

The Migration Industry

While unofficial networks are responsible for a high proportion of immigration and employment, the scale of flows has also created something of a commercial "migration industry" that provides many of the same services. This is not a new phenomenon. Since the times of slavery, workers have been shipped to where they are needed. At times of rapid economic growth, European countries have set up recruitment offices to boost the supply of volunteers.

State-Linked Emigration

Nowadays, however, most of the organizing is done in the sending countries. In some cases governments themselves have taken a hand. A number of Asian governments, aware of the potential benefits of immigration both in relieving unemployment and as a source of income through remittances, have been actively promoting emigration. Governments can collect some of this income from taxes, but they also gain from various other fees, including passport fees and travel taxes.[18]

Of the Asian sending countries, Viet Nam has in the past exerted the tightest control. Before the collapse of communism in Eastern Europe, Vietnamese public corporations entered into labor-supply agreements with Eastern European governments. At one point in the late 1980s, this involved over 60,000 workers. Many of these have now been repatriated and the Vietnamese government is looking for alternative markets. China too has organized emigration through state-owned corporations. In 1994, the Ministry of Foreign Trade and Economic Cooperation reported that there were 200,000 migrant workers abroad, mostly on labor-service agreements or employed by one of the fifty-six national government corporations that had overseas construction contracts—an estimated 30,000 were reportedly employed in 1995 building a new airport in Hong Kong (China).[19] The Republic of Korea during the 1980s used its national work force to complete construction contracts abroad, but also recruited workers for foreign employers through the state-owned Korean Overseas Development Corporation.[20]

In other countries, state involvement has been more through co-operation with, and regulation of, the private sector. The Philippines, for example, attempted to follow the Korean recruitment model but eventually settled for licensing and supervising recruitment agencies through the Philippine Overseas Employment Agency. Licensed agencies have to fulfill minimum capital requirements, pay annual licensing fees, and follow a complex set of regulations. The government has also established a procedure for remittances, and requires that migrants send a certain proportion of their income through the official system—from 50 to 70 percent for land-based workers.[21] Other governments, by contrast, play a relatively small part in sending workers overseas. In Bangladesh, Pakistan, and Sri Lanka in 1993, less than 2 percent of workers depended on public agencies.[22]

Labor Brokers

Many workers travel independently, but an increasing proportion nowadays use labor brokers. The check-in queues at Dhaka airport in Bangladesh are regularly thronged by long lines of expectant immigrants neatly kitted out in the uniforms of labor contractors who have recruited them en masse for jobs in Malaysia or the Persian Gulf. Over recent decades, the development of the international labor market has created a whole new recruitment industry in both sending and receiving countries that—for a fee—will offer to find work and arrange many details such as passports, visas, transport, and accommodation.

This can soak up a high proportion of the emigrants' income. In the Philippines, for example, recruiters are legally allowed to charge migrants 5,000 pesos ($192). In practice, they often charge up to 120,000 pesos for employment in Japan, or 100,000 pesos for Taiwan (China).[23] The situation is similar in Thailand. The Thai Ministry of Labor stipulated in 1995 that the maximum fee payable to brokers was the equivalent of $2,240, but hundreds of Thai workers in Taiwan (China) interviewed by the *Bangkok Post* said they had paid far in excess of this.[24] Generally, migrants pay three to four months' salary up front—though in some cases much more—money they usually have to borrow by mortgaging their houses or land. In Bangladesh, for example, workers can pay up to $2,000 to get to Saudi Arabia as unskilled laborers—more than 80 percent of their expected annual earnings.[25] Similar fees are demanded by brokers elsewhere. In the Czech Republic, for example, which in 1996 had around 250,000 foreign workers, mostly from Eastern Europe, one Ukrainian worker employed for $2.50 per hour reported that he had to pay half his wages to a broker.[26]

Migrant Trafficking

Some brokers do little more than put employers and workers in contact, but others are involved in illegal trafficking—often transporting people over vast distances, and arranging to bribe many officials en route, from airline workers to immigration officers. At the destination, they may also arrange accommodation. In Europe in 1993, some 15–30 percent of undocumented immigrants were thought to have used the services of traffickers. In the case of asylum applicants, the proportion is even higher—20 to 40 percent make use of traffickers for all or part of their journeys.

Trafficking is an increasingly complex business. As part of one of the first attempts to analyze the various stages in the process, Salt and Stein produced the diagram shown in Figure 9.1.[27] Trafficking is a very lucrative enterprise. An organized trip over an East European border, or a boat trip from Morocco to Spain, would be worth about $500, but a sophisticated travel package from China to the United States can cost up to $30,000. Globally, trafficking is thought to bring in $5–7 billion per year.[28] As governments discover the routes, they try to crack down on this trade, but traffickers usually manage to keep one step ahead. As one route closes, another opens. In the early 1990s, for example, thousands of Chinese were discovered arriving in the United States by ship. Now they seem to have switched to more complex routes. In 1996, the U.S. Immigration and Naturalization Service announced that it had broken up an organization that smuggled hundreds of undocumented Asians into the United States through a route that included the Russian Federation, Cuba, and Central America. Chinese, Indian, and Pakistani migrants paid up to $28,000 each for a grueling clandestine journey that reached its climax in the Mexican town of Reynosa, from which teenagers ferried them across the Rio Grande to McAllen, Texas, on inner tubes.[29]

This illegal flow of workers has created a large market for forged documents. Bangkok has developed into a major production center—particularly for emigrants from China. Passports, mainly Korean and Japanese, are sent from many parts of the world, where they are suitably amended. These forgeries demand very sophisticated technology (the latest Japanese passport has the holder's picture imprinted on the cover) and sell for up to $2,000 each.[30] This service is readily available from travel agencies who advertise in Bangkok's Chinese-language newspapers. The traffickers also provide false work contracts. In Spain, for example, traffickers have set up ghost companies to issue work contracts that enabled would-be immigrants from the Dominican Republic to obtain legal visas.

Figure 9.1 The Trafficking Business

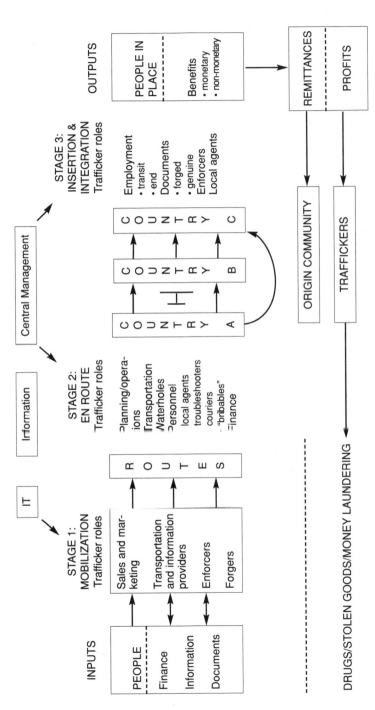

Source: Salt, J., and J. Stein, 1997.

Many people also lubricate the flow of migrants by offering financing. In many cases, this will be a long-term loan to set against earnings, but shorter-term finance is also available. Bolivian peasants who want to enter Argentina as "tourists," for example, are required to demonstrate their bona fides by showing to immigration officials that they have the equivalent of $1,500 in spending money. This has created a new form of financial intermediary, demanding what must be a world-record interest rate. For the hour or so it takes to cross the border, bus companies and others will lend migrants the necessary cash—for a 10 percent fee.[31]

Transnational Communities

Immigrants often maintain strong ties with their homes—and in so doing are creating new kinds of transnational communities. Often migrants from a particular town or village will establish an organization to fund projects back home. The hamlet of San José de la Paz Arriba, twenty miles south of San Salvador, for example, lives almost entirely off money sent from relatives in the United States. Expatriates have set up a committee in Los Angeles to help pay for community projects: the streets have been paved and a new clinic constructed using the donations.[32] In France, immigrants from Mali come predominantly from the Kayes region and the majority of these are members of the forty or so development associations that have contributed, among other things, to the development of hydraulic networks to improve agricultural production.[33] Many similar organizations have been established between Mexico and the United States—indigenous Mixtec migrants who have moved to California and Oregon have established associations to promote self-help and raise money for community development projects for their villages.[34]

In other cases, immigrants have established businesses that arise directly out of their transnational existence. Many small businesses in the Dominican Republic are run by returned emigrants who have maintained contacts in the United States—and frequently travel abroad. Sometimes their return visits are to look for new investors, often with the help of Dominican-owned financial and real estate agencies in New York. But on other occasions they can just be on sales trips. What may look like migrants loaded up with gifts may actually be garment makers carrying finished clothes in one direction and textiles and other materials back again.

Particularly well traveled are the Otovalan Indians from Ecuador, whose transnational communities have penetrated major cities of Europe and North America where they sell colorful clothing imported from their home community. Many men have taken European wives, who eventually return to Ecuador with them—where they may be seen in Ecuadorian towns wearing traditional costume.[35]

New kinds of community have also been created by flows of immigrants from East Asia to the West Coast of North America. This has produced what are called "astronauts"—Chinese entrepreneurs who make their living commuting by air across the Pacific.[36]

These transnational links are also of interest to governments of sending countries. In the past, they have often been discouraged by autocratic governments that saw emigrants as a potential focus of opposition. Before democratization, the government of Cape Verde, for example, was suspicious of emigrant groups and had overseas embassy staff monitor their activities and intervene in immigrant organizations.[37]

So valuable have these transnational links become that governments of sending countries are now anxious to institutionalize and nurture relationships with emigrants. At various times, and to varying degrees, these have included Colombia, Haiti, India, the Republic of Korea, Mexico, Portugal, Paraguay, and a number of West Indian states. Portugal, for example, has around 2,000 Portuguese associations in different countries around the world, and the Portuguese government offers financial support and equipment, particularly for young people, to sustain Portuguese language and culture. Every four years it convenes a world congress of representatives of these communities, usually attended by the prime minister.[38]

In 1990 the Mexican government established the Program for Mexican Communities Abroad. This represented something of a policy sea change. Previously, the Mexican elite had looked down on emigrants to the United States, referring to them as *pochos*—a derogatory term that implies they had separated from their roots, and lost themselves in a country without history or tradition. Now the idea is to consider them as part of a wider Mexican nation. This change in attitude is partly a reaction to the surprisingly large numbers of Mexicans who applied for legal U.S. residence as a result of the 1996 U.S. Immigration Reform and Control Act. Among other things, the program has been used for lobbying during NAFTA, and for setting up more cultural links to home communities.[39]

India's Non-Resident Indian (NRI) program, which started in the early 1980s, was more an attempt to tap emigrants' wallets. After India started to liberalize its economy and to welcome inward investment, the country's 10 million people abroad (650,000 of them in the United States) were seen as a source of finance because many were active entrepreneurs and maintained close contacts with India. In the past, Indians too have rejected those who have gone overseas (in the nineteenth century, Indians who went abroad were obliged to undergo elaborate purification rituals when they returned). The NRI program still has to deal with some of these suspicions—as well as some new ones. There is resentment, for example, at the construction of elaborate new hospitals that cater to NRIs when they are in India.[40]

The intensification of communications links is likely to promote further transnational communities. Migrants nowadays can develop and maintain many kinds of links, constructing social networks and life-worlds that join them to two or more locations and nation-states. This is a reality that is increasingly being explored in fiction.[31] For these communities, concepts of culture and society can no longer be linked simply to territory or geography.

Conclusion

Once set in motion, international migration develops a momentum of its own and is supported by a complex web of networks—private, commercial, and governmental. Now that both mass and personal communications are so widely available at a global level, international migration has become a less expensive and less traumatic option. Globalization, by reducing both the financial and the emotional costs of moving, will ensure that such networks are strengthened and extended.

Notes

1. Smith, A. 1776, p. 24.
2. Stalker, P. 1994, p. 31.
3. *Migration News,* vol. 4, no. 1.
4. Subervi, F., cited in Rohter, L. 1996.
5. International Telecommunications Union. 1995, p. 12.
6. World Bank. 1998b, p. 291.
7. Robberson, T. 1995.
8. Rodríguez, N. 1996.
9. Dumon, W. 1989, p. 256.
10. Jasso, G., and M. Rosenzweig. 1994.
11. Goza, F. 1994, p. 144.
12. Durand, J., and D. Massey. 1992, p. 24.
13. Casillas, R. 1996, p. 164.
14. Wilpert, C. 1992.
15. Waldinger, R. 1996b, p. 271.
16. Waldinger, R. 1996a.
17. Mattei, L. 1996, p. 42.
18. Abella, M. 1995, p. 9.
19. *Migration News,* vol. 2, no. 2.

20. Hyun, O.-S. 1989, p. 151.
21. Goss, J., and B. Linquist. 1995, p. 340.
22. Ghosh, B. 1996, p. 86.
23. Silverman, G. 1996.
24. Janchitfah, S. 1995.
25. Abella, M. 1995, p. 15.
26. *Migration News*. vol. 4, no. 1.
27. Salt, J., and J. Stein. 1997, p. 491.
28. Widgren, J. 1994.
29. Dillon, S. 1996.
30. Gooi, K. 1996.
31. Escobar, G. 1996.
32. Robberson, T. 1995.
33. Libercier, M., and H. Schneider. 1996, p. 38.
34. Smith, M. 1994, p. 27.
35. Portes, A.1996, p. 25.
36. Portes, A. 1997, p. 813.
37. Libercier, M., and H. Schneider. 1996, p. 45.
38. Abella, M. 1997, p. 88.
39. Smith, R. 1993.
40. Lessinger, J. 1992, p. 53.
41. Connell, J. 1995.

10

The Demand for Immigrants

The logic of standard economic theory dictates that if international disparities flatten out, in the long term the demand for mass migration should tail off. But there may be reasons international migration could persist for some time to come. To examine these, it is useful to look more closely at the reasons people move. A number of explanatory models have been proposed for international migration. Some emphasize "push" factors from the sending countries, while others underline the "pull" factors from the receiving ones. Some look at individual motivation, whereas others look at the structures within which people make their migration decisions. The main theories include:[1]

Neoclassical economic theory. This theory considers differences in the supply and demand for labor in sending and receiving countries, and sees workers moving in response to higher wage rates. Neoclassical theory can also be applied at the individual level—workers are seen as moving to maximize the returns on their "human capital." As explored in earlier chapters, it is largely this theory that suggests that globalization, by causing economies to converge, will eventually reduce migration.

New economics of migration. This theory argues that migration arises not from individual choice but decisionmaking by groups, usually families or households. Sending one or more members overseas not only increases the immediate group income, but it also diversifies its sources of earnings, thus offering some kind of insurance. If globalization, and particularly liberalization, further reduce the stability of employment, they may make households feel even less secure—and increase the need to spread their risks.

Dual labor market theory. This argues that migration is not some intermediate phase, but has become a permanent and necessary feature of modern industrial societies. Capitalism, it is argued, will always need people who are willing to work in unpleasant conditions and who will accept precarious employment. This enables firms to operate flexibly—laying people off or reemploying them as required. Nationals have become increasingly educated and have rising aspirations, and are often unwilling to accept these conditions—even preferring to live off welfare payments. Immigrants, on the other hand, especially those who do not intend to stay, are less choosy and take what they can get. Theoretically, this problem could be solved by improving wages and conditions for "inferior" jobs, but this would be socially very disruptive, and could lead to inflation, so employers prefer the easier (and cheaper) option of employing immigrant labor.

World-systems theory. All the above theories and mechanisms have also been incorporated into what is called "world-systems theory." This is not really a separate model, but rather a description of how flows of capital, goods, and labor fit together and are interlinked. Instead, seeing migration as the result of the characteristics of individual economies ascribes to it a dramatic influence of the capitalist penetration of rich economies into poor, creating a total world system. In the poor countries, such penetration destroys traditional sources of income and simultaneously creates a pool of mobile labor, part of which is driven to migrate internationally. Capitalist expansion facilitates such flows by developing communication and transport links.

In addition to these theories, which suggest why migration is likely to commence, numerous other mechanisms have been proposed to explain the volume and character of flows. As described in previous chapters, these include the creation of migrant networks, and the intervention of recruitment agencies and other institutions that promote migration.

Most of these explanations are complementary—even if they operate at different levels. One can, for example, consider a Mexican laborer moving to the United States as having made an individual decision encouraged by friends or family. But he or she can also be seen as responding to broad structural forces—the collapse of agrarian employment in Mexico, on one side, and a shortage of fruit pickers in California, on the other.

The Persistence of the Dual Labor Market

Of these theories, the least optimistic in terms of reducing international migration is the dual labor market theory. It does indeed appear that the demand for immigrants is structurally embedded into many societies. In many respects, globalization seems likely to increase the number of undesirable or precarious jobs. This is the result of a degree of polarization. Although many new highly paid jobs are being created at the top of the labor market, many of the old white- and blue-collar jobs are being automated out of existence, while more people are being drawn into lower-paid employment in services. This is part of a longer-term trend toward informalization and casualization of lower-paid employment.[2]

It is in precisely this area that immigrants have long filled the gap—working for wages that national workers reject and doing the "dirty, dangerous, and difficult" jobs. Some indication of the relative importance of these factors can be gained from Figure 10.1, which summarizes the results of a survey of employers in the Netherlands in 1994.[3] This shows the reasons that eighty-four employers from a range of industries gave for employing undocumented immigrants. The most important was that legal employees cost too much, particularly in the garment industry and in catering. But employers also said it was difficult to find people prepared to work for short periods to meet production peaks, particularly in agriculture, or to do work that was physically hard or dirty.

Figure 10.1   Reasons for Employing Workers Without Authorizations, Netherlands, 1994

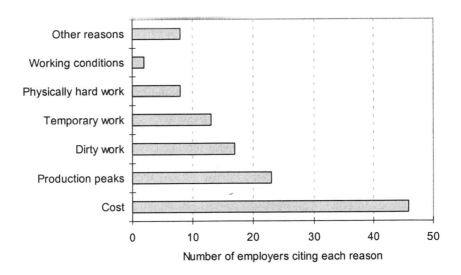

Source: Zandvliet, C., and J. Gravesteijn-Ligthelm, 1994.

One sector that has long relied on casual labor for unpleasant tasks is construction. Rising levels of education in Southeast Asia, for example, combined with the availability of more attractive options, dissuade local people from working on construction sites. The Republic of Korea has made determined efforts to exclude unskilled foreign workers, but still needs them for construction: in late 1996, the Ministry of Construction and Transportation admitted that it would have to import more foreign labor to build the country's first high-speed railway line. Similarly, Malaysia, another country that has vowed to reduce its dependence on foreign workers, still employed some 25,000 foreigners to work on the new Kuala Lumpur International Airport. In Argentina, those working on construction sites are often undocumented immigrants from Chile or Brazil: a Brazilian worker can earn ten times as much by working in Argentina.[4]

It might be possible to tempt more people to work by raising wages, but it is clear that, given the opportunity of employing foreigners, employers are unwilling to do this. In Germany in 1996, for example, unemployment was above 12 percent, and there were around 200,000 unemployed German construction workers. Yet at the same time, Germany was employing around 500,000 foreign construction workers—including 100,000 from the United Kingdom. The issue is largely one of salaries. British workers, who might have earned $12 an hour at home, could earn $25 in eastern Germany. German workers, on the other hand, by the time the legal wage and all the benefits have been paid, might cost $35 per hour. Moreover, as one employer told the *New York Times,* the advantage of foreigners is that "they have no family, no hobbies, so they can work through the weekend."[5]

In some cases it may be possible to eliminate immigrant jobs through mechanization. In Malaysia, for example, where gasoline (or petrol) pumps are largely operated by Bangladeshi attendants, the government decreed that from 1997 all pumps should convert to self-service—even though this was more expensive than having people work around the clock. But many other tasks, particularly in service industries, are impossible to mechanize.

Moreover, the range of jobs that nationals reject seems to be widening. Taxi driving in the United States, for example, was until about ten years ago a fairly respected blue-collar job. Nowadays, few native workers will drive taxis and this has rapidly become an "immigrant job." In Washington, D.C., the Taxi Operators' Association estimated in 1996 that over the previous twenty-five years the proportion of drivers who were foreign-born rose from 25 to 85 percent.[6]

As well as being needed at the bottom of the labor market, immigrants are also needed at the top. Industrial countries, under pressures of international competition, also have a strong demand for highly skilled labor. Bringing in the best and the brightest foreign workers also helps keep the United States at the leading edge of new technology. When proposals were made for an immigration bill to reduce the category of visa that enabled the employment of skilled foreigners, one of the loudest protests came from Microsoft chairman Bill Gates, who said: "If you want to prevent companies like ours from doing work in the United States, this [bill] is a masterpiece."[7]

Industrial countries are left, therefore, with a demand for immigrant labor at the top and bottom of the job spectrum. This can be expressed graphically, as in Figure 10.2. A similar diagram can be produced for the United States, though the base is much broader because there is a greater demand for unskilled labor.[8]

The Demographic Factor

A further factor creating and sustaining immigrant jobs in the years ahead could be demographic change—and specifically the aging of industrial societies. Families are having fewer children. In 1990–1995, the average total fertility rate of the more developed regions

Figure 10.2 Patterns of Skill Supply and Demand, Western and Northern Europe, 1990

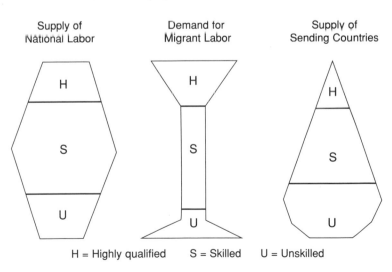

Supply of National Labor	Demand for Migrant Labor	Supply of Sending Countries

H = Highly qualified   S = Skilled   U = Unskilled

Source: Böhning, W., 1995.

was 1.68 children per woman, well below the 2.1 children per woman required for long-term replacement. Nine countries had average fertility levels of 1.5 or less children per woman, with the lowest rates in Italy (1.2), Spain (1.3), and Germany (1.3).[9]

This is raising a number of concerns—in particular that dependency ratios will increase as a shrinking working population is obliged to support an expanding elderly one. For the OECD countries as a whole, over the period 1990–2005, the proportion of the population aged sixty-five and over has been projected to rise from 18.9 to 22.3 percent. The highest proportions of the elderly in 2005 will be reached by Japan, 29.2 percent; Greece, 28.6 percent; and Italy, 28.3 percent.[10]

Could immigration provide a solution? It certainly does have an impact on population growth. Between 1990 and 1995, for the industrial countries as a whole, net immigration was responsible for 45 percent of overall population growth (1.8 out of 4.0 per 1,000).[11] What is less certain is that immigration will help make the population more youthful. In the postwar period in the United Kingdom, for example, immigration increased the total population by around 3 million, yet had little impact on the age structure.[12] The problem is that although newly arriving immigrant families often have higher fertility rates than natives of the country, they rapidly take on the characteristics of the rest of the population.

In countries with declining fertility, it would take large numbers of immigrants just to maintain stable populations and even more to maintain acceptable dependency ratios. One study looked at the alternatives for four countries: Austria, Belgium, Canada, and Spain. Just to achieve a numerically stable population, Canada by 2025 would need to be absorbing 120,000 per year, and Belgium 40,000. Spain would need 100,000 immigrants per year from 2010. But to guarantee a minimum dependency ratio of three working adults to every elderly person would require much greater influxes—over 170,000 annually for Belgium and Austria, and 700,000 for Canada and Spain.[13]

In these circumstances, and especially when many of the native population are unemployed, a better option would be to try to increase fertility—which some countries such as Sweden have succeeded in doing—and to encourage a higher proportion of the existing population to work.[14] No country is likely to use immigration on anything like a sufficient scale to offset fertility declines.

Nevertheless, the aging society may still have a direct impact on immigration—by increasing the demand for health-care workers. The U.S. Bureau of Labor has predicted that between 1996 and 2006 health-care services will increase by 30 percent and account for 3.1

million new jobs, the largest numerical increase of any industry.[15] Because these are professions that typically have a high proportion of immigrant workers, the demand for foreign-trained nursing personnel will remain strong.

Conclusion

Industrial countries will probably have an irreducible requirement in the years ahead for the kind of employment that immigrants are willing to undertake. Indeed, if globalization expands the number of jobs at the bottom of the employment scale, particularly in services, it could well increase the demand for their labor. This prospect is not inevitable. Both states and enterprises could choose to improve salaries and working conditions to make certain jobs more attractive to national workers. But given the nervousness even about setting minimum wages, this seems unlikely to happen on any significant scale, leaving most industrial countries with an irreducible demand for some immigrant workers.

Notes

1. Massey, D., et al. 1993, p. 431.
2. Sassen, S. 1996, p. 584.
3. Zandvliet, C., and J. Gravesteinjn-Ligthelm. 1994.
4. Werna, E. 1997, p. 7.
5. Andrews, E. 1996,
6. Glass, S. 1996, p. 21.
7. Mills, M. 1995.
8. Böhning, W. 1995.
9. United Nations Population Division. 1996.
10. OECD. 1994, p. 24.
11. United Nations Population Division. 1996.
12. Coleman, D. 1995, p. 155.
13. Wattelar, C., and G. Roumains. 1991, p. 62.
14. Coleman, D. 1992, p. 455.
15. U.S. Bureau of Labor Statistics. 1998.

11

A Question of Time

Industrial countries are always likely to want cheap immigrant labor to do the jobs that national workers refuse. But the supply could dry up if closer and deeper integration of economies promotes economic development in poorer countries that eventually blunts the incentive to emigrate.

This development could take some time. The first and most basic issue is that of scale. Between 1995 and 2025, the labor force of the low-income countries is set to grow from 1.4 billion to 2.2 billion.[1] Neither trade nor investment at their current levels will be at a sufficient level to absorb this expansion. Globalization may help indirectly, by exposing poorer economies to competition, spurring productivity, and generally stimulating their economies to grow more rapidly. But in terms of direct impact, neither trade nor investment is a sufficient answer.

Beyond this, there are serious problems of distribution. If globalization is to have a greater impact on immigration, it will have to proceed in a more even and egalitarian fashion. Thus far, it has been very lopsided—with the greatest benefits going to countries already ahead in the race. Many poor countries have, for example, so far seen very little of the expansion of world trade. The least-developed countries, with 10 percent of world population, have only 0.3 percent of world trade—and that is half the proportion of two decades ago. Similar imbalances are evident in the flows of foreign direct investment. These are concentrated in industrial countries and faster-growing parts of the developing world: 70 percent of the world's population gets only 10 percent of global investment. All of this is further skewing international incomes. While global per capita income tripled over the period 1960–1994, there are now a hundred countries with per capita incomes lower than in the 1980s, or in some cases lower than in the 1970s or 1960s.[2]

Globalization may in the end not flatten international disparities but merely re-sort countries into new categories of rich and poor. Sub-Saharan African countries, for example, have yet to feature very strongly on intercontinental migration trails, but the exodus toward South Africa, and the flows of Africans moving through the fairly relaxed border controls of Eastern Europe, could be a harbinger of things to come.

Moreover, even if globalization does make some countries as a whole richer, it could heighten internal disparities. India, say, or China, which between them have the majority of the world's poor people, might become much more integrated into the global economy. This could still leave vast numbers of their people marginalized—but with sufficient resources to travel overseas in search of work.

Finally, there is the question of time. Even given the most optimistic assumptions, there is little doubt that as development proceeds, migration pressure will rise in the decades ahead. This additional flow of emigrants might represent a temporary hump—as history would suggest. But there is no guarantee that history will repeat itself. Posterity may have other ideas. The poorest developing countries are trying to industrialize in a fiercely competitive environment. In a world of winners and losers, the losers do not simply disappear, they seek somewhere else to go. What could be a temporary hump could develop instead into a steep and relentless ascent.

Notes

1. World Bank. 1996, p. 9.
2. UNDP. 1997.

Bibliography

Abella, M. 1991. *Workers to Work or Work to the Workers*. Bangkok: ILO, mimeographed.

————. 1994. "International Migration in the Middle East: Patterns and Implications for Sending Countries," in *International Migration: Regional Processes and Responses*, Economic Studies no. 7, Geneva, United Nations Economic Commission for Europe.

————. 1995. "Policies and Institutions for the Orderly Movement of Labour Abroad." International Migration Papers, no. 5. Geneva: ILO.

————. 1997. *Sending Workers Abroad*. Geneva: ILO.

Abella, M., and Y.-b. Park. 1994. "Labour Shortages and Foreign Workers in Small Firms of the Republic of Korea," in *Adjustments to Labour Shortages and Foreign Workers in the Republic of Korea*, International Migration Papers, no. 1. Geneva: ILO.

Abowd, J., and R. Freeman. 1991. "Introduction and Summary," in J. Abowd and R. Freeman (eds.), *Immigration, Trade and the Labor Market*. Chicago: University of Chicago Press.

ACP-EU Courier. 1996. "Colossal Loss of Investments for Developing Countries," no. 159, September-October.

Adepojou, A. 1995. "Migration in Africa: An Overview," in J. Baker and T. Aina (eds.), *The Migration Experience in Africa*. Uppsala, Sweden: Nordisk Afrikainstitutet.

Agence-France-Presse. 1996. "RP Workers Remit Billions." *The Nation* (Bangkok), 24 September.

Alburo, F. A. 1994. "Trade and Turning Points in Labor Migration." *Asian and Pacific Migration Journal* 3, no. 4.

Andrews, E. 1996. "The Upper Tier of Migrant Labor." *New York Times*, 11 December.

Appadurai, A. 1990. "Disjuncture and Difference in the Global Cultural Economy," in M. Featherstone (ed.), *Global Culture: Nationalism, Globalization and Modernity*. London: Sage.

Appleyard, R. 1991. *International Migration: Challenge for the Nineties*. Geneva: International Organization for Migration (IOM).

Arnold, F. 1992. "The Contribution of Remittances to Economic and Social Development," in M. Kritz et al. (eds.), *International Migration Systems: A Global Approach*. Oxford: Clarendon Press.

Asiaweek. 1991. "Where Have All the Nurses Gone?" 30 August.

Atkinson, R. 1996. "200-Year-Old Ties Pull Ethnic Germans Back." *Washington Post*, 31 March.

Avila, J. 1998. "Regional Economic Integration and International Migration: The Case of NAFTA." Paper prepared for the Technical Symposium on International Migration and Development. United Nations ACC Task Force on Basic Social Services for All. The Hague.

Bairoch, P. 1996. "Globalization Myths and Realities: One Century of External Trade and Foreign Investment," in R. Boyer and D. Drache (eds.), *States Against Markets: The Limits of Globalization*. London: Routledge.

Bangladesh Bureau of Statistics. 1995. *Report on Labour Force Survey, 1990–91*. Dhaka: Bangladesh Bureau of Statistics.

Barnet, J., and J. Cavanagh. 1994. *Global Dreams: Imperial Corporations and the New World Order*. New York: Simon & Schuster.

Baum, J. 1995. "Toil and Trouble." *Far Eastern Economic Review*, 25 May.

Belluck, P. 1995. "Healthy Korean Economy Draws Immigrants Home." *New York Times*, 22 August.

Bennett Jones, O. 1996. "Millions Cross Ex-Soviet Borders." *The Guardian*, 23 May.

Bergsman, J., and X. Shen. 1995. "Foreign Direct Investment in Developing Countries: Progress and Problems." *Finance and Development*, December.

Bhagwati, J., and M. Rao. 1996. "The U.S. Brain Gain: At the Expense of Blacks?" *Challenge*, March.

Blanco Fdez. de Valderrama, C. 1993. "The New Hosts: The Case of Spain." *International Migration Review* 27, no. 1.

Böcker, A. 1995. "Migrant Networks: Turkish Migration to Western Europe," in R. van der Erf and L. Heering (eds.), *Causes of International Migration*. Luxembourg: Eurostat.

Böhning, W. 1995. "Top and Bottom End Labour Import in the United States and Europe: Historical Evolution and Sustainability." International Migration Papers, no. 8. Geneva: ILO.

Böhning, W., and N. Oishi. 1995. "Is International Economic Migration Spreading?" *International Migration Review* 29, no. 3.

Borjas, G. 1994. "The Economics of Immigration." *Journal of Economic Literature* 32.

Branigan, W. 1995. "Importing Skills Needed, or Cheap Labor?" *Washington Post*, 21 October.

Bratsberg, B., and D. Terrell. 1996. "Where Do Americans Live Abroad?" *International Migration Review* 30, no. 3.

Brown, R. 1995. "Consumption and Investment from Migrants' Remittances in the South Pacific." International Migration Papers, no. 2. Geneva: ILO.

Brzezinski, M. 1995. "No Through Road to the West." *The Guardian*, 13 June.

Bulman, R. 1996. "Apparel Workers Stranded as Plant Moves to Mexico." *The Journal of Commerce*, 24 September.

Bureau of Immigration Research. 1996. *Immigration Update, March Quarter*. Canberra.

Butcher, K., and D. Card. 1991. "Immigration and Wages: Evidence from the 1980s." *American Economic Review* 81, no. 2.

Camp, S. 1990. *Cities: Life in the World's Largest Metropolitan Areas*. Washington, DC: Population Action International.

Carrington, W., and P. de Lima. 1996. "The Impact of 1970s Repatriates from Africa on the Portuguese Labour Market." *Industrial and Labour Relations Review* 49, no. 2.

Casillas, R. 1996. "The Mexican Dilemma," in A. Simmon (ed.), *International Migration, Refugee Flows and Human Rights in North America: The Impact of Trade and Restructuring.* New York: Center for Migration Studies.

Castles, S., R. Iredale, and E. Vasta. 1994. "Australian Immigration: Between Globalization and Recession." *International Migration Review* 28, no. 2.

Citizenship and Immigration Canada. 1997. "Staying the Course: Annual Immigration Plan." URL: http://www.cicnet.ci.gc.ca/english/pub/anrep97e.html.

Coleman, D. 1992. "Does Europe Need Immigrants?" *International Migration Review* 26, no. 2.

———. 1995. "International Migration: Demographic and Socioeconomic Consequences in the United Kingdom and Europe." *International Migration Review* 29, no. 1.

Connell, J. 1995. "Samoan Worlds, Culture, Migration, Identity and Albert Wendt," in R. King, J. Connell, and P. White (eds.), *Writing Across Worlds: Migration and Literature.* London: Routledge.

Connell, J., and R. Brown. 1995. "Migration and Remittances in the South Pacific: Towards New Perspectives." *Asian and Pacific Migration Journal* 4, no. 1.

Cornelius, W., and P. Martin. 1993a. "The Uncertain Connection: Free Trade and Rural Mexican Migration to the United States." *International Migration Review* 27, no. 3.

———. 1993b. *The Uncertain Connection: Free Trade and Mexico-U.S. Migration.* Center for U.S.-Mexican Studies, University of California, San Diego.

Cose, E. 1992. *A Nation of Strangers: Prejudice, Politics, and the Populating of America.* New York: William Morrow.

Department of Immigration and Multicultural Affairs. 1998. Government of Australia. URL: http://www.immi.gov.au/facts/02keyfac.htm.

Dicken, P. 1992. *Global Shift: The Internationalization of Economic Activity.* London: Paul Chapman.

Dillon, S. 1996. "Asian Aliens Now Smuggled from Mexico," *New York Times,* 30 April.

Drogin, B. 1996. "Post-Apartheid South Africa Targets Illegal Immigrants." *Washington Post,* 7 October.

Dumon, W. 1989. "Family and Migration." *International Migration* 28, no. 2.

Dunn, A. 1995. "Skilled Asians Leaving U.S. for High-Tech Jobs at Home." *New York Times,* 21 February.

Dunning, J. 1993. *Multinational Enterprises and the Global Economy.* Wokingham, UK: Addison-Wesley.

Durand, J., and D. Massey. 1992. "Mexican Migration to the United States: A Critical Review." *Latin American Research Review* 27, no. 2.

Durand, J., E. Parrado, and D. Massey. 1996. "Migradollars and Development: A Reconsideration of the Mexican Case." *International Migration Review* 30, no. 2, p. 423.

Economic and Social Commission for Western Asia (ESCWA). 1993. "Arab Labour Migration to the Gulf: Size, Impact and Major Policy Issues." Paper presented at the Expert Group Meeting on Population Distribution and Migration. New York: United Nations, mimeographed.

Economic Council of Canada. 1991. *New Faces in the Crowd: Economic and Social Impacts of Immigration.* Ottawa: Economic Council of Canada.

Economist, The. 1993a. "Rural Revolution." 13 February.

———. 1993b. "Strawberries and Circuit Boards." 27 March.

———. 1994. "You Ain't Seen Nothing Yet." 1 October, survey, p. 29.

———. 1995a. "Latin America in the Fallout Zone." 7 January.

———. 1995b. "Putting Mexico Together Again." 4 February.

———. 1995c. "Managing on the Frontier." 24 June.

———. 1995d. "Only Communicate." 24 June.

———. 1995e. "The New Trade in Humans." 5 August.

———. 1995f. "The Profits of Sin." 12 August.

———. 1996a. "Bits and Bytes." 9 March.

———. 1996b. "The Lost Daughters." 11 May.

———. 1997. "One World?" 18 October.

———. 1998a. "Miracle or Mirage?" 11 April.

———. 1998b. "What Would Confucius Say Now?" 25 July.

Engardio, P. 1994. "The Skills Explosion: High-Tech Jobs All over the Map." *Business Week,* 18 November.

ERCOMER, 1997. "The World-Wide Web Virtual Library—Migration and Ethnic Relations." URL: http://www.ercomer.org/wwwvl/.

Ernst, D., and P. Guerrieri. 1998. "International Production Networks and Changing Trade Patterns in East Asia: The Case of the Electronics Industry." *Oxford Development Studies* 26, no. 2.

Escobar, G. 1996. "Free Trade Leads to Mobile Labor as Bolivians Seek Jobs in Argentina." *Washington Post,* 15 September.

European Commission. 1994. "Growth, Competitiveness and Employment: The Challenges and Ways Forward into the 21st Century." White Paper. Brussels: European Commission.

Faini, R., and A. Venturini. 1993. "Trade, Aid and Migrations: Some Basic Policy Issues." *European Economic Review* 37.

———. 1994. "Migration and Growth: The Experience of Southern Europe." Centro Studi Luca d'Agliano/Queen Elizabeth House Development Studies Working Papers, no. 75. Turin/Oxford.

Far Eastern Economic Review. 1994. "Filipinos First—Or Last?" 13 January.

Fassmann, H., and R. Münz. 1994. "European East-West Migration, 1945–1992." *International Migration Review* 28, no. 3.

Federici, N. 1989. "Causes of International Migration," in R. Appleyard (ed.), *The Impact of International Migration on Developing Countries.* Paris: OECD.

Findlay, A. 1994. "An Economic Audit of Contemporary Immigration," in S. Spencer (ed.), *Strangers & Citizens: A Positive Approach to Migrants and Refugees.* London: IPPR/Rivers Press.

Fischer, P., and T. Straubhaar. 1996. "Is Migration into EU Countries Demand Based?" in *Economics and European Union Migration Policy.* London: Institute for Public Policy Research.

Fix, M., and J. Passel. 1994. *Immigration and Immigrants: Setting the Record Straight.* Washington, DC: Urban Institute.

Freeman, R. 1993. "Immigration from Poor to Wealthy Countries: Experience of the United States." *European Economic Review* 37.

Frey, W. H. 1994. "The New White Flight." *American Demographics,* April.

Friedman, T. 1996. "Big Mac I." *New York Times,* 10 December.

Fuentes, N., et al. 1993. "Local Sourcing and Indirect Employment: Multinational Enterprises in Northern Mexico," in P. Bailey et al. (eds.), *Multinationals and Employment: The Global Economy of the 1990s.* Geneva: ILO.

Gabbard, S., R. Mines, and B. Boccalandro. 1994. "Migrant Farmworkers: Pursuing Security in an Unstable Labor Market." ASP Research Report 5. Washington, DC: U.S. Department of Labor.

Ghosh, B. 1996. "Economic Migration and the Ending Countries," in J. van den Broeck (ed.), *The Economics of Labour Migration*. Cheltenham, UK: Edward Elgar.

Gilbert, A. 1994. "Human Resources: Work, Housing and Migration." Paper prepared for the Independent Commission on Population and the Quality of Life, Paris, 1994; mimeographed.

Glass, S. 1996. "Taxis and the Meaning of Work." *The New Republic*, 5 August.

Gooi, K. 1996. "Citizenship for a Price." *The Nation* (Bangkok), 30 September.

Goss, J., and B. Lindquist. 1995. "Conceptualizing International Labour Migration: A Structuration Perspective." *International Migration Review* 29, no. 2.

Goza, F. 1994. "Brazilian Immigration to North America." *International Migration Review* 28, no. 1.

Grassman, S. 1980. "Long-Term Trends in Openness of National Economies," *Oxford Economic Papers* 32. Oxford: Clarendon Press.

Gray, P. 1994. "Looking for Work? Try the World." *Time*, 19 September.

Griffin, K., and T. McKinley. 1994. "A New Framework for Development Cooperation." Human Development Report Office, Occasional Papers, no. 11. New York: UNDP.

Hanson, G., and A. Spilimbergo. 1996. "Illegal Immigration, Border Enforcement, and Relative Wages: Evidence from Apprehensions at the U.S.-Mexico Border." National Bureau of Economic Research Working Paper no. 5592. Cambridge, MA.

Hatton, T., and J. Williamson. 1998. *The Age of Mass Migration: Causes and Economic Impact*. New York: Oxford University Press.

Head, K., and J. Ries. 1998. "Immigration and Trade Creation: Econometric Evidence from Canada." *Canadian Journal of Economics* 31, no. 1.

Hinojosa Ojeda, R. 1994. "The North American Free Trade Agreement and Migration," in OECD, *Migration and Development: New Partnerships for Cooperation*. Paris.

Hiro, D. 1992. *Black British, White British*. London: Paladin.

Hirst, P., and G. Thompson. 1996. *Globalization in Question*. Cambridge: Polity Press

Hobsbawm, E. 1994. *Age of Extremes: The Short Twentieth Century*. London: Michael Joseph.

Hollifield, J. 1992. *Immigrants, Markets and the State: The Political Economy of Post-War Europe*. Cambridge, MA: Harvard University Press.

Hoon, S. J. 1995. "Investment Going Global." *Far Eastern Economic Review*, 2 November.

Hopper, J. 1995. "Troops Seal Europe's Back Door." *The Guardian*, 11 May.

Huntingdon, S. 1996. "The West Unique, Not Universal." *Foreign Affairs* 75.

Huntoon, L. 1998. "Immigration to Spain: Implications for a Unified European Union Immigration Policy." *International Migration Review* 32, no. 2.

Hyun, O.-S. 1989. "The Impact of Overseas Migration on National Development: The Case of the Republic of Korea," in R. Amjad (ed.), *To the Gulf and Back*. Geneva: ILO.

IGC. 1999. "Intergovernmental Consultations on Asylum, Refugee and Migration Policies in Europe, North America and Australia." URL: http://www.igc.ch/.

Iglebaek, O. 1995. "The Baltic Connection." *Refugees*, no. 101. Geneva: UNHCR.

ILO. 1992. *World Labour Report*. Geneva.

———. 1994. *World Labour Report*. Geneva.

———. 1995. *World Employment 1995.* Geneva.

———. 1996. *World Employment 1996/97.* Geneva.

———. 1998. "The Social Impact of the Asian Financial Crisis." Technical report for discussion at the High-Level Tripartite Meeting on Social Responses to the Financial Crisis in East and Southeast Asian Countries, April 1998, Bangkok.

IOM (International Organization for Migration). 1994. "Trafficking in Migrants: Characteristics and Trends in Different Regions of the World." Paper presented at the 11th IOM Seminar on Migration, Geneva; mimeographed.

ITU (International Telecommunication Union). 1995. *World Telecommunication Development Report.* Geneva.

Janchitfah, S. 1995; "Taking Risks Abroad." *Bangkok Post,* 8 October.

Jasso, G., and M. Rosenzweig. 1994. "Labour Immigration to the United States," in OECD, *Migration and Development: New Partnerships for Cooperation.* Paris.

Jehl, D. 1996. "For Kuwaitis, Self-Reliance Proves an Elusive Goal." *New York Times,* 24 September.

Kazi, S. 1989. "Domestic Impact of Overseas Migration: Pakistan," in R. Amjad (ed.), *To the Gulf and Back.* Geneva: ILO.

Khan, A. 1994. *Overcoming Unemployment.* Geneva: ILO.

Kim, J.-Y. 1995. "Korean Emigrés return to Chase Economic Dreams." *Bangkok Post,* 17 October.

Kochan, N. 1996. *The World's Greatest Brands.* New York: Interbrand/Macmillan Business.

Kopinak, K. 1996. "Household, Gender and Migration in Mexican Maquiladoras: The Case of Nogales," in A. Simmons (ed.), *International Migration, Refugees Flows and Human Rights in North America: The Impact of Trade and Restructuring.* New York: Center for Migration Studies.

Krugman, P., and A. Venables. 1994. "Globalization and the Inequality of Nations," Centre for Economic Policy Research, Discussion Paper no. 1015, London.

Layard, R., et al. 1992. *East-West Migration: The Alternatives.* Cambridge, MA: MIT Press.

Lessinger, J. 1992. "Investing or Going Home? A Transnational Strategy Among Indian Immigrants in the United States," in N. Schiller et al. (eds.), *Towards a Transnational Perspective on Migration.* New York: Annals of the New York Academy of Sciences, vol. 645.

Libercier, M., and H. Schneider. 1996. *Migrants: Partners in Development Cooperation.* Paris: OECD.

Lim, L. 1993. "Growing Economic Interdependence and Its Implications for International Migration." Paper presented at the Expert Group Meeting on Population Distribution and Migration, Santa Cruz, Bolivia.

Mahmood, R. 1996. "Labour Crunch, Foreign Workers and Policy Responses: The Experience of Japan." *International Migration* 34, no. 1.

Mahmud, W. 1989. "The Impact of Overseas Labour Migration on the Bangladesh Economy: A Macro-Economic Perspective," in R. Amjad (ed.), *To the Gulf and Back.* Geneva: ILO.

Martin, P. 1991. *The Unfinished Story: Turkish Labour Migration to Western Europe.* Geneva: ILO.

———. 1993. *Trade and Migration: NAFTA and Agriculture.* Washington, DC: Institute for International Economics.

Martin, P., and E. Midgley. 1994. "Immigration to the United States: Journey to an Uncertain Destination." *Population Reference Bureau Population Bulletin* 49, no 2.

Martin, P., and J. Taylor. 1996. "Managing Migration: The Role of Economic Policies." Paper presented at the Migration Policy in Global Perspective conference at the New School, New York; mimeograph.

———. 1996. "The Anatomy of a Migration Hump," in OECD, *Development Strategies, Employment and Migration: Insights from Models.* Paris.

Massey, D. 1988. "Economic Development and International Migration in Comparative Perspective." *Population and Development Review* 14, no. 2.

Massey, D., et al. 1993. "Theories of International Migration: A Review and Appraisal." *Population and Development Review* 19, no. 1.

———. 1994. "An Evaluation of International Migration Theory: The North American Case." *Population and Development Review* 20, no. 4.

Mattei, L. 1996. "Gender and International Labour Migration: A Networks Approach." *Social Justice* 23, no. 3.

McDonald, H. 1992. "India's Silicon Valley." *Far Eastern Economic Review,* 10 December.

Mehrländer, U. 1994. "The Development of Post-War Migration and Refugee Policy," in Institute for Public Policy Research, *Immigration as an Economic Asset.* London.

Migration News. Various issues. URL: http://www.migration.ucdavis.edu.

Miles, R. 1997. "Investors Spurn UK's Threadbare Rag Trade." *The Guardian,* 15 February.

Miller, M. 1998. "New Gold Mountain." *Far Eastern Economic Review,* 9 July.

Miller, R. 1993. "Determinants of U.S. Manufacturing Investment Abroad." *Finance and Development,* March.

Millman, J. 1996. "Following the Immigrants." *Forbes,* 1 January, p. 38.

Mills, M. 1995. "Gates Assails Bill to Curb Immigration." *Washington Post,* 29 November.

Minnaar, A., et al. 1995. "Who Goes There? Illegals in South Africa." *Indicator SA* 12, no. 3.

Minnaar, A., and M. Hough. 1996. *Who Goes There? Perspectives on Clandestine Migration and Illegal Aliens in Southern Africa.* Pretoria: HSRC Publishers.

Morgan Stanley & Co. Inc. 1996. "The Great Global Restructuring Debate." *U.S. Investment Research,* 11 October.

Münz, R., and R. Ulrich. 1998. "Germany and Its Immigrants: A Socio-Demographic Profile." *Journal of Ethnic and Migration Studies* 24, no. 1.

Navaretti, G., and G. Perosino. 1992. "Redeployment of Production, Trade Protection and Global Firm Strategy: The Case of Italy." Centro Studi Luci d'Agliano/Queen Elizabeth House, Working Paper no. 55. Turin/Oxford.

Nayyar, D. 1989. "International Labour Migration from India: A Macro-Economic Perspective," in R. Amjad (ed.), *To the Gulf and Back.* Geneva: ILO.

———. 1997. "Emigration Pressures and Structural Change: Case Study of Indonesia." International Migration Papers, no. 20. Geneva: ILO.

OECD (Organization for Economic Cooperation and Development) 1994. *The OECD Jobs Study: Evidence and Explanations, Part I.* Paris, p. 4.

Ohmae, K. 1996. *The End of the Nation-State: The Rise of Regional Economics.* London: HarperCollins.

Oman, C. 1994. *Globalisation and Regionalisation: The Challenge for Developing Countries.* Paris: OECD, p. 17.

Ong, P., L. Cheng, and L. Evans. 1992. "Migration of Highly Educated Asians and Global Dynamics." *Asian and Pacific Migration Journal* 1, nos. 3–4.

Oxfam, 1996. *Trade Liberalization as a Threat to Livelihoods: The Corn Sector in the Philippines.* Oxford.

Pang, E. 1993. *Regionalization and Labour Flows in Pacific Asia.* Paris: OECD.

Parisotto, A. 1993. "Direct Employment in Multinational Enterprises in Industrialized and Developing Countries in the 1980s: Main Characteristics and Recent Trends," in P. Bailey et al. (eds.), *Multinationals and Employment: The Global Economy of the 1990s.* Geneva: ILO.

Park, Y.-b. 1991. "Foreign Labour in Korea: Issues and Policy Options." Paper presented at the second Japan-ASEAN Forum on International Labour Migration in East Asia, Tokyo, United Nations University/ILO; mimeographed.

Peterson, M. 1998. "Languages of Globalization: Modernity and Authenticity," in *Proceedings of the Fifth AUC Research Research Conference,* Cairo, the American University in Cairo.

Portes, A. 1996. "Global Villagers." *The American Prospect,* no. 25.

———. 1997. "Immigration Theory for a New Century: Some Problems and Opportunities." *International Migration Review* 31, no. 4.

Pritchett, L. 1996. "Forget Convergence: Divergence Past, Present, and Future." *Finance and Development,* June.

Reitzes, M. 1995. "Divided on the 'Demon': Immigration Policy Since the Election." *Policy, Issues and Actors* (Johannesburg, Centre for Policy Studies) 8, no. 9.

Rifkin, J. 1995. *The End of Work.* New York: Tarcher/Putnam.

Robberson, T. 1995. "Migration Grows, Heads South as Well as North." *Washington Post,* 18 September.

Robertson, R. 1992. *Globalization: Social Theory and Global Culture.* London: Sage.

Rodríguez, N. 1996. "The Battle for the Border: Notes on Autonomous Migration, Transnational Communties and the State." *Social Justice* 23, no. 3.

Rodrik, D. 1997. *Has Globalization Gone Too Far?* Washington, DC: Institute for International Economics.

Rohter, L. 1996. "In Spanish, It's Another Story," *New York Times,* 15 December.

———. 1997. "Blows from NAFTA Batter the Caribbean Economy." *New York Times,* 30 January.

Roy, A. 1997. "Job Displacement Effects of Canadian Immigrants by Country of Origin and Occupation." *International Migration Review* 31, no. 1.

Saith, A. 1997. "Emigration Pressures and Structural Change: Case Study of the Philippines." International Migration Papers, no. 19. Geneva: ILO.

Salt, J. 1996. "Economic Developments Within the EU: The Role of Population Movements," in D. Corry (ed.), *Economics and European Union Migration Policy.* London: Institute for Public Policy Research.

Salt, J., and J. Stein. 1997. "Migration as a Business: The Case of Trafficking." *International Migration* 35, no. 4.

Samuel, J. 1995. "Temporary and Permanent Labour Immigration into Canada: Selected Aspects." International Migration Papers, no. 10. Geneva: ILO, p. 11.

Sandoval, M. 1996. "Immigrants Needed in California Fields; INS Knows It." *National Catholic Reporter,* 28 June.

Sassen, S. 1988. *The Mobility of Labour and Capital.* Cambridge: Cambridge University Press.

———. 1996. "New Employment Regimes in Cities: The Impact on Immigrant Workers." *New Community* 22, no. 4.

Sauvant, K., P. Mallampally, and P. Economou. 1993. "Foreign Direct Investment and International Migration." Paper presented at the Conference on Migration and International Cooperation, Paris, OECD; mimeographed.

Scalabrini Migration Center. 1996. URL: http://www.sequel.net.

———. 1999. *Asian Migration Atlas 1999.* URL: http://www.scalabrini.asn.au/atlas/amatlas.htm.

Schlosser, P. 1995. "In the Strawberry Fields." *Atlantic Monthly,* November.

Silverman, G. 1996. "Vital and Vulnerable." *Far Eastern Economic Review,* 23 May.

Smith, A. 1776. *An Inquiry into the Nature and Causes of the Wealth of Nations,* Oxford: Oxford World Classics Edition, Oxford University Press, p. 74.

Smith, M. 1994. "Transnational Migration and the Globalization of Grass-Roots Politics." *Social Text* 39.

Smith, R. 1993. "Deterritorialized Nation Building: Transnational Migrants and the Reimagination of Political Community by Sending States." Paper presented at the seminar on Migration and the State, New York University, Center for Latin American and Caribbean Studies, New York, May; mimeographed.

SOPEMI (Système d'observation permanente des migrations)/OECD. Various years. *Trends in International Migration.* Paris.

Stahl, C. 1995. "Theories of International Labour Migration: An Overview." *Asian and Pacific Migration Journal* 4, nos. 2–3.

Stahl, C., and A. Habib. 1991. "Emigration and Development in South and Southeast Asia," in G. Papademetriou and P. Martin (eds.), *The Unsettled Relationship: Labour Migration and Economic Development.* Westport, CT: Greenwood Press.

Stalker, P. 1994. *The Work of Strangers: A Survey of International Labour Migration.* Geneva: ILO.

———. 1997. *The Dancing Horizon: Human Development Prospects for Bangladesh.* Dhaka: United Nations.

Stansell, J. 1990. "Space—The Final Dustbin." *The Observer,* 24 November.

Stanton R. S. 1992. "Migrant Remittances and Development." Paper presented at the 10th IOM Seminar on Migration, Geneva.

Stanton, R. S., and M. Teitelbaum. 1992. "International Migration and International Trade." World Bank Discussion Paper no. 160, Washington, DC.

Stark, O. 1992. "Migration in Developing Countries: Risk, Remittances and the Family." World Employment Programme Working Paper, MIG WP. 58. Geneva: ILO.

Stevenson, R. 1996. "NAFTA's Impact on Employment Is Slight, Study Says." *New York Times,* 19 December.

Summers, L. 1995. "Ten Lessons to Learn." *The Economist,* 23 December.

Sussangkarn, C. 1996. "Labour Market Developments and International Migration in Thailand," in *Migration and the Labour Market in Asia: Prospects to the Year 2000.* Paris: OECD.

Swan, N., et al. 1991. *Economic and Social Impacts of Immigration.* Ottawa: Economic Council of Canada.

Tapinos, G. 1994. "The Macroeconomic Impact of Immigration: Review of the Literature Published Since the Mid-1970s," in *Trends in International Migration.* Paris: SOPEMI/OECD.

Taylor, J. 1996. "Labour Market and Fiscal Impacts of Immigration." International Migration Papers, no. 10. Geneva: ILO.

Teilhard de Chardin, P. 1955. *The Phenomenon of Man.* London: Collins.

Thomas-Hope, E. 1998. "Releasing the Development Potential of Return Migration: The Case of Jamaica." Paper prepared for the Technical Symposium on International Migration and Development. United Nations ACC Task Force on Basic Social Services for All. The Hague.

Thornton, E. 1995. "What Shortage?" *Far Eastern Economic Review,* 25 May.

Tirschwell, P. 1996. "Frozen Out by Free Trade." *The Journal of Commerce,* 1 March.

Tzeng, R. 1995. "International Labor Migration Through Multinational Enterprises." *International Migration Review* 29, no. 1, p. 139.

UNCTAD (United Nations Conference on Trade and Development). 1994. *World Investment Report.* Geneva.

———. 1996a. *Trade and Development Report.* Geneva.

———. 1996b. *World Investment Report.* Geneva.

UNDP (United Nations Development Programme). 1994. *Empowerment of Women: UNDP's Report on Human Development in Bangladesh.* Dhaka.

———. 1996, 1997. *Human Development Report.* New York.

———. 1998. *Overcoming Human Poverty: UNDP Poverty Report 1998.* New York.

UNESCO (United Nations Educational, Scientific and Cultural Organization). 1994. "TV Transnationalization: Europe and Asia." Reports and Papers on Mass Communications, no. 109. Paris, p. 79.

UNFPA (United Nations Population Fund). 1993. *The State of World Population.* New York.

UNHCR (United Nations High Commissioner for Refugees). 1995. "Asylum Under Threat." *Refugees* (Geneva), no. 101.

United Nations. 1994. *World Urbanization Prospects: The 1994 Revision.* New York: United Nations Population Division.

———. 1994, 1997. *World Economic and Social Survey.* New York.

United Nations Population Division. 1996. *World Population Prospects: The 1996 Revision* (annex tables).

———. 1997. *World Population Monitoring, 1997.* New York.

United Press International. 1996. "Mexican Deportees Report Good Treatment," 21 April.

UNRISD (United Nations Research Institute for Social Development). 1995. *States of Disarray: The Social Effects of Globalization.* Geneva.

U.S. Bureau of Labor Statistics. 1998. *Occupational Outlook Handbook, 1998–99.* URL: http://www.stats.bls.gov/oco/oco2003.htm.

U.S. Immigration and Naturalization Service. Various years. *Statistical Yearbook of the Immigration and Naturalization Service.* Washington, DC: U.S. Department of Justice.

———. 1998.URL: http://www.ins.usdoj.gov/stats/index.html.

Vatikiotis, M. 1994. "The Lure of Asia." *Far Eastern Economic Review,* 3 February.

Vernez, G., and K. McCarthy. 1996. *The Costs of Immigration to Taxpayers: Analytical and Policy Issues.* Santa Monica: Rand Corporation, MR-705-FF/IF.

Waldinger, R. 1996a. "The Jobs Immigrants Take." *New York Times,* 3 November.

———. 1996b. "Who Makes the Beds? Who Washes the Dishes?" in H. Duleep and P. Wunnava (eds.), *Immigrants and Immigration Policy: Individual Skills, Family Ties, and Group Identities.* Greenwich, CT: JAI Press.

Waters, M. 1996. *Globalization*. London: Routledge.

Watkins, K. 1997. "Globalization and Liberalization: Implications for Poverty, Distribution, and Inequality." Human Development Report Office, Occasional Paper no. 32. New York: UNDP.

Wattelar, C., and G. Roumains. 1991. "Simulations of Demographic Objectives and Migration," in *Migration: The Demographic Aspects*. Paris: OECD.

Wentsz, L. 1996. "World Brands." *Ad Age International,* September, p. 121.

Werna, E. 1997. "Labour Migration in the Construction Industry in Latin America and the Caribbean." Sectoral Activities Programme Working Paper. Geneva: ILO.

Werner, H. 1996. "Economic Integration and Migration: The European Case," in J. van den Broeck (ed.), *The Economics of Labour Migration*. Cheltenham, UK: Edward Elgar.

Widgren, J. 1994. "International Response to Trafficking in Migrants and the Safeguarding of Migrant Rights." Paper presented at the 11th IOM Seminar on Migration, Geneva; mimeographed.

Williamson, J. 1995. "The Evolution of Global Labour Markets Since 1830: Background Evidence and Hypotheses." *Explorations in Economic History* 32.

———. 1996. "Globalization, Convergence, and History." *The Journal of Economic History* 56, no. 2.

Wilpert, C. 1992. "The Use of Social Networks in Turkish Migration to Germany," in M. Kritz et al. (eds.), *International Migration Systems: A Global Approach*. Oxford: Clarendon Press.

Wong, D. 1997. "Transience and Settlement: Singapore's Foreign Labor Policy." *Asian and Pacific Migration Journal* 6, no. 2.

Wood, A. 1994. *North-South Trade, Employment and Inequality*. Oxford: Clarendon Press.

World Bank. 1993, 1995, 1996. *World Development Report*. Washington, DC.

———. 1994. *Bangladesh: From Stabilization to Growth*, Report No. 12724-BD.

———. 1998a. *Global Development Finance*. Washington, DC.

———. 1998b. *World Development Indicators*. Washington, DC.

World Commission on Culture and Development. 1995. *Our Creative Diversity,* Paris: UNESCO.

World Trade Organization. 1999. *World Merchandise Exports by Region and Selected Economies*. Geneva. URL: http://www.wto.org/wto/statis/web_pube.xls.

Yang, Y. 1996. "Safeguarding the Future of World Trade in Textiles and Clothing." Economics Division Working Papers, Development Issues, 96/1, Australian National University, Canberra.

Yang, Y., and C. Zhong. 1996. "China's Textile and Clothing Exports in a Changing World Economy." Economics Division Working Papers, East Asia 96/1, Australian National University, Canberra.

Zabin, C., and S. Hughes. 1995. "Economic Integration and Labour Flows: Stage Migration in Farm Labor Markets in Mexico and the United States." *International Migration Review* 29, no. 2.

Zandvliet, C., and J. Gravesteijn-Ligthelm. 1994. *Illegal Employment in the Netherlands: Extent and Effects*. A study commissioned by the Ministry of Social Affairs and Employment and the Ministry of Justice. The Hague.

Zimmerman, K. 1993. "Industrial Restructuring, Unemployment and Migration," in L. Bekemans and L. Tsoulakis (eds.), *Europe and Global Economic Interdependence*. Brussels: European Interuniversity Press.

———. 1994. "The Labour Market Impact of Immigration," in S. Spencer (ed.), *Immigration as an Economic Asset*. London: Institute for Public Policy Research.

Zlotnik, H. 1998. "The Dimensions of International Migration." Paper prepared for the Technical Symposium on International Migration and Development, United Nations ACC Task Force on Basic Social Services for All. The Hague.

Index

About the Book

Globalization is one of the dominant themes of the past decade—causing alarm, excitement, or merely resignation. The flows of trillions of dollars through financial exchanges, the intensification of international competition, the potential for global economic instability—all have gripped the world's attention.

But all of this has had surprisingly little to do with the movement of people. Discussions of globalization rarely consider international migration at all—or they deal with it as a residual category, an afterthought.

Yet migration, or the potential for migration, is a central part of globalization. *Workers Without Frontiers* by Peter Stalker helps redress the balance. This new book from ILO shows how migration connects with movements of goods and capital, and how it is closely tied up with other social and economic changes.

Will globalization lead to economic convergence that will eventually cause migration pressures to subside, or will the years of upheaval that lie ahead release new migrant flows? Bringing together the latest information on international migration, *Workers Without Frontiers* offers a unique assessment of a complex and contentious issue.